POSITIONING FOR

Architecture and Design Firms

POSITIONING FOR

Architecture and Design Firms

JACK REIGLE

WILEY

John Wiley & Sons, Inc.

This book is printed on acid-free paper. ♾

Copyright © 2011 by John Wiley & Sons, Inc. All rights reserved.

Published by John Wiley & Sons, Inc., Hoboken, New Jersey.
Published simultaneously in Canada.

For general information on our other products and services, or technical support, please contact our Customer Care Department within the United States at 800-762-2974, outside the United States at 317-572-3993 or fax 317-572-4002.

Wiley also publishes its books in a variety of electronic formats. Some content that appears in print may not be available in electronic books.

For more information about Wiley products, visit our Website at http://www.wiley.com.

Library of Congress Cataloging-in-Publication Data:

Reigle, Jack.
  Positioning for architecture and design firms / by Jack Reigle.
      p. cm.
  ISBN 978-0-470-47225-5 (cloth); ISBN 978-0-470-91869-2 (ebk);
  ISBN 978-0-470-91870-8 (ebk); ISBN 978-0-470-91871-5 (ebk);
  ISBN 978-0-470-95029-6 (ebk); ISBN 978-0-470-95054-8 (ebk)
  1. Architectural services marketing. 2. Design services–Marketing. 3. Market segmentation.
  I. Title.
  NA1996.R36 2011
  720.68–dc22   2010025644

Printed in the United States of America

10 9 8 7 6 5 4 3 2 1

CONTENTS

PREFACE

After I completed my previous book, *Silver Bullets: Strategic Intelligence for Better Design Firm Management*, I knew there was more to put in writing. Once I determined that the positioning topic was ripe for exploration and development, I approached John Czarnecki, senior acquisitions editor at John Wiley & Sons, about the idea, and we proceeded on our way. There was one small bump in the road, however. We initially discussed the concept for this book in September of 2008—the same moment when the entire world seemed to be collapsing around us, economically speaking. Clearly, the outline I had developed for the positioning book didn't take into account enough about a future that very suddenly seemed in tremendous peril.

The more I spoke with clients, and heard and read the accounts of firms attempting to make it through the storm, the more I knew that we should wait. When more daylight and perspective were available, we would all be able to see the situation more clearly. That time arrived after the summer of 2009. There was a change in tone and an uptick in confidence, albeit only because the economy had survived so far. What was confirmed for many people as 2009 came to a close was that we were in for a long, uphill struggle. The world hadn't ended, but the end appeared to be close enough to shake loose all but a few basic expectations and beliefs.

Reembarking on the positioning book in late 2009, I discovered that a wealth of new perspectives was indeed developing. Firm leaders were sorting through any number of critical choices, in addition to keeping their firms alive and breathing.

As I thought more deeply about the positioning topic, I realized that it filled a significant gap between strategic planning, where I had been spending most of my time, and the daily tasks of the firm's projects and business functions. I could then reimagine the topic of positioning not just as a word that seems interchangeable with strategy or marketing, but as a real issue that firm leaders needed to focus on. One of the dangers of strategy is that it gets dragged down too quickly by the demands of daily production on projects, and loses its meaning. This realization led me to see the positioning activity as a bridge between strategy and the real life of projects, not merely as another word that gets used in generalizations.

Waiting for the clouds to clear also aided the "how to" aspects of this book, which were always part of the plan. All of the cases included here were developed after the crisis period had passed, so I'm hopeful that readers looking for new ideas or for confirmation of their own ideas will appreciate the willingness of the case contributors to share their stories.

When I look back on my original outline for this book, prepared in August 2008, it's clear to me how much my perspective has been adjusted. While many aspects of the original material do appear here, the context and emphasis have shifted markedly. I'm not a pessimist or skeptic at heart, but something tells me the process still has a long way to go—for our country, the design industry, and ourselves as individuals. Thank you for taking the time to read the fruits of my labor, and I sincerely hope you'll find a few good ideas here that can help along the way.

Jack Reigle
Palm Beach Gardens, Florida

ACKNOWLEDGMENTS

Having been a part of the design industry for 20 years, as a strategy and organizational consultant, I have learned the most from the clients I've worked with and for. Their professional dedication, stellar work ethic, and probing questions have taught me about myself, and provided a remarkable platform for my consulting and writing endeavors. My thanks to each of them for allowing me to share in their journey.

I knew that I wanted to include a significant number of case studies in the book, so I reached out to a few colleagues to assist with that process. My thanks go to Mike Reilly of Reilly Communications in Boston, Massachusetts, for his contribution of the Bioengineering Group case study. Similar gratitude goes to Terry Casey for her contribution of the GeoDesign case. Her business is On Target Marketing & Communications in the Hartford, Connecticut, area, and, like Mike Reilly, she runs a public relations consulting firm with a focus on design and construction. The KPS Group case came about through Cliff Moser, FAIA, of CADFORCE, Inc. Cliff was kind enough to point me to a member of his firm's alliance network, and lo and behold, the KPS Group case study became the quintessential case story of recent times for many design firms.

My continued thanks to Ellen Flynn-Heapes, SPARKS founder and developer of the Framework Assessment tool. Much of the writing in the chapter on firm identity and purpose is based on her previous contributions.

I want to thank John Czarnecki, senior acquisitions editor at John Wiley & Sons, for working with me. My thanks also go to Seema Michon, who assisted me with any number of administrative and organizational tasks as I raced to complete the manuscript.

I wish to express my deepest appreciation to my wife, Yvonne, who was unwavering in her support of this effort, and as patient as anyone could be as I spent nights and weekends holed up with my computer or simply gazing skyward for inspiration.

And to other family and friends I've neglected or lost touch with during this trek, I do apologize, and look forward to engaging with you again soon!

INTRODUCTION

As we prepare to enter the second decade of the twenty-first century, the unease of the past few years remains with us. While the financial system didn't completely collapse, and overall economic signs suggest a nascent recovery, much of what has been seen as "business as usual" is no longer evident. Companies have made large cutbacks in staff, expansion plans, and expenses. The government has taken unprecedented steps to prop up the economy, add jobs, and begin to deal with the systemic entanglements that led to the near meltdown. Many previous downturns were characterized as "inventory-driven"; companies had become overconfident and had overproduced, requiring a period of adjustment to rebalance the system. In those terms, the office glut of the late '90s and the dot-com bust of the new millennium were relatively isolated blips on the screen of economic health. Not so this time.

Within this context, the design and construction industry has been among the hardest hit. Canceled and delayed projects have resulted in layoffs, office closings, severe spending reductions, and a greater sense of uncertainty than most firm owners have ever experienced. Even with a number of projects moving ahead, there are relentless cash flow issues. Problems collecting receivables have led to the inability to meet payroll, and many firms have found it necessary to shop for new banking relationships as lending standards have tightened.

Survival has been the word for recent times, and the harshness of the situation for most firms cannot be overstated. Yet, in the middle of this storm, many firms are beginning to find their footing. With a combination of bold decisions, practical expectations, and a belief that they can turn this phase into an opportunity, they are moving ahead with new plans, strategies, and programs. They are reassessing their position in the marketplace with clear-eyed pragmatism born of necessity and a determination to endure as both business entities and contributors to society.

In the first chapter of this book, "Future Tense," we explore the larger context for considering the state of our times and the generational cycles that are shaping the next major phases. Although many ideas are being written, blogged about, and presented as the latest ways to make it through the uncertainty, very often the best answers don't come from experimentation but from viewing the situation with clarity and with commitment to one's original mission. What would you have done differently if you had known that your business would be cut in half in 2009? Would you have turned down work in the good years? Would you have chosen different markets and clients? And now that the challenge of the future has arrived in full force, are you being shaped by the issues at hand, or are you determined to fulfill the purpose you defined long ago—albeit within changed circumstances? A tense future will remain with us for quite a while, if current readings are accurate. Remaking many of the structures of our economy and society will be arduous, and historic decisions will have to be made. As this process unfolds, the Boomers will be winding down their careers and relinquishing their dominant role in society. A new generation will be stepping in to take over the reins, and they will be faced with many difficult choices. One thing that's certain is that this new generation will think and act differently as leaders and problem solvers. They will be responsible for helping resolve the long-term effects of the recent crisis, or for actively managing new phases of greater crises, if they arrive. This role will lead to a more practical view of the world and how to proceed. A new pragmatism will be on display, focused on results as opposed to grand experimentation or risks. With over 500 years of history pointing to this next generational phase, we might consider surrendering any remnants of the idea that recent occurrences will blow over and all will be back to normal soon.

The term "positioning," while familiar to us all, has been loosely applied in most industries. Its strictest application has been in the consumer product markets, where branding and messaging have become an art form indispensable to the science of volume and pricing. In the second chapter of this book, appropriately called "Positioning," we define positioning for design firms as comprehending a macro-view of the firm and the marketplace. As stated in the Preface, positioning isn't just another word for marketing strategy; it's a holistic, systems-driven viewpoint and approach that firms need to add to their business-planning arsenal. Positioning is the tool to use to create the critical alignment between strategic planning and operations, and to keep that alignment intact. If strategy is the picture window of the firm's future, positioning comprises the panes within that window that define, stabilize, and manage the entire view.

Strong strategic positioning relies heavily on a firm's ability to develop and maintain its identity in the marketplace. The third chapter of the book, "Firm Identity and Purpose," provides the foundational material and tools firms can use to make these choices and to create the essential framework for developing their positioning program. The SPARKS Framework Assessment, provided in the Appendix, organizes these crucial choices and decisions into six primary archetypes. It provides perspective on the importance of a firm's operating model, allowing for sturdier development of key business functions as well as greater control over the firm's infrastructure and systems. Although defining a firm's purpose is a very individual consideration, we explore it as a baseline methodology that provides the perspective firms and leaders need to rise above the fray of competition, as well as to construct highly rewarding and satisfying careers.

Chapter 4, "Markets and Services," follows, showing how firms can make decisions to implement core positioning strategies. Whether it's a new or strengthened service offering, a decision to expand geographically, or a model for developing deeper market expertise, these decisions embody the firm's ability to fulfill the promise of their purpose. The chapter includes a number of case studies that profile real firms and leaders in their quest for their strongest positioning alternatives and outcomes. We also investigate the topic of design fees and commoditization, a lingering problem for the industry that must be addressed more effectively through stronger firm positioning.

Chapter 5, "The Marketing System," provides a detailed view of many of the core elements of marketing that every firm needs to develop. Some of these are traditional elements such as proposals, speaking and writing for recognition, and the like. Others, such as the explosion of social media, may be new to many firms, while public relations is an area typically needing more attention and creativity to make it most effective. Positioning and the marketing aspects within that context are systems problems to be solved, not simply tasks to be completed. A firm that recognizes the importance and power of a holistic approach to developing and managing these vital functions will be able to fulfill their potential in a much more effective and efficient manner.

The sixth chapter, "Organizational Development," discusses a fundamental imperative that is a traditional weakness within the design industry. Whether it's due to concerns about overhead, lack of information, or simply the demands of running an unfocused consultancy, many organization-related initiatives remain unexplored or overlooked—yet, successful positioning relies heavily on the right organizational design, in good times or bad. Smart firms are taking the opportunity to rethink their approach to this need, within the scope of the lingering uncertainties around us, and are acting to effect important changes that move beyond cost savings. Is your firm one of them?

"Advanced Research and Open Innovation" is the final chapter, and it provides a view of methodologies for raising a firm's game by means of a stronger leadership position based on ideas, trends, collaboration, and the creative process. Competition will continue to increase over the coming years, and the speed of change will accelerate again and again. New networks of experts and learners are forming every day to explore ways to capitalize on the latest technologies and approaches that will feed the machinery of the design industry for many years to come. Each firm needs to find the right connections to these nearly invisible forces around us, participating in and contributing to the advancement of the industry, for the ultimate benefit of the firm and of society as a whole.

The Appendix contains the aforementioned SPARKS Framework Assessment instrument. It can provide firms with the essential elements of discussion and choice necessary to determine their core identity. With that as a starting point, firms can build strategy, vision, purpose, and the ultimate positioning plan needed to guide their development on a more holistic level through the coming years.

This book comes at a time when the world is still lurching from a fairly violent shock. It's easy to believe that we're still in a wait-and-see mode, that we should hunker down, watch the cash flow, try reviving a few small projects to get through the next year. With history as a guide, however, we see that nothing could be further from the truth. Now is the time to act, and to make the types of changes in thinking and approach that only a crisis can inspire. Hopefully, this book's big-picture themes, combined with practical how-to examples, will lead many readers to explore a new vision for transforming their firms, preparing them for the long march into one of the most challenging periods of modern times.

POSITIONING FOR

Architecture and Design Firms

CHAPTER 1

FUTURE TENSE

THE BIG SHIFT

One way to view the events of the past few years is to recognize that the future is now upon us. It's a bit more uncertain than we expected. "Future tense" means that the next 10 years will deliver more larger-than-life anxieties, significant changes, surprises, and sharp edges than we've been used to. The era of normal is over. And despite all the talk about a "new normal," it will take a while to arrive. The United States, along with most of the civilized world, has undergone a system failure unfamiliar to all but those of quite advanced age and scientifically improbable memories. The list of culprits has now become familiar: global climate change, terrorism, economic excess, federal debt burdens, the opacity of the bond markets, demographic shifts, and the sense that these disasters are bearing down on us all at once. Few industries and professions are flourishing, and many are braced for aftershocks that are yet to arrive.

As this wave has washed over us, many thinkers and theorists have weighed in on what it is, what it means, and how we should plan for the future. Looming larger than most among this group is a team from the Deloitte Center for the Edge (DCE), a division of Deloitte Touche Tohmatsu. John Hagel III, John Seely Brown, and Lang Davison (we'll call them HBD), who lead the enterprise, are prolific authors, bloggers, and speakers exploring this new territory of what they call the Big Shift. DCE conducts original research and develops substantive points of view for new corporate

1

growth. Its aim is to help senior executives make sense of and profit from emerging opportunities on the edge of business and technology. The Center focuses on the boundary, or edge, of the global business environment, where strategic opportunity is the highest. From a business perspective, the philosophies espoused by the HBD trio include embracing the opportunity offered by the evolving environment, increasing the speed of learning, acting boldly to seize the moment, and accepting an overarching goal of changing the world. As indicated by the group's name, the concept of "the edge" is important to think about. As new patterns emerge from the chaos, edges are the areas of high potential—for the economy, for professions, and for individuals. Emerging economies form a geographic edge, as do new generations of people. Technology has an edge, perhaps best identified by new, rapidly growing social media tools and connections. The "core," in contrast, is where the financial power and other resources reside. This includes the U.S., Japan, and Western Europe from the geographical perspective, and the aging Boomer population from a demographic point of view. At the firm level, the core is the accumulative value in the marketplace represented by experience, capabilities, and main revenue sources. For individuals, the core is primarily represented by personal and professional relationships.

According to HBD, the patterns that begin to be recognizable as change occurs are those where "the edge transforms the core." Edge-dwellers tend to be explorers and risk takers who band together with other like-minded thinkers and doers. There is more willingness to share information and insights with others out on the edge. Yet there is initially a limited inertia within the edge, because mature, traditional institutions are in the core and maintain control over resources, customers, and profits. The edge and core have a strong need to reach out and connect, yet many barriers prevent this from happening easily and efficiently. One provocative thought brought forward by HBD reverses the common approach of disruption theory, which would say that in order to participate in this overall dynamic, a firm would bring the edge to the core. Instead, they suggest bringing the core to the edge, exposing your organization to innovations, new management practices, and new tools that emerge on that edge. Of course, choosing the edges to participate in, to invest in, and ultimately to use to transform your business is the big decision. Each firm needs to spend time deciding which edges represent a potentially new platform that, over time, could be utilized to design and implement new initiatives. From a design industry perspective, a few edges are already visible. Integrated Project Delivery (IPD) represents a significant shift for many firms, and when pursued to its highest form, transforms the client experience and the whole of project performance. Building Information Modeling (BIM) holds the same promise, and is gaining more traction every year. Social media growth among design firms, although generally lagging behind that of other industries, is also gaining significant acceptance that should accelerate rapidly as the new decade unfolds.

These three edges are already visible and moving ahead within the design industry, but others are out there and deserve exploration. Within the sustainability movement, these may take the form of diverse collaborative teams seeking to innovate for new materials, develop more effective building products, or research new methodologies for tracking and measuring building performance.

With all this progress on edge-related thinking, some readers may believe that the job's done, but that thought is a dangerous one. The speed and quality of implementation mean everything to IPD and BIM. A firm that installs a new system but doesn't utilize it to its fullest, or collaborate with forward-thinking partners, will remain in the back of the pack as the edge takes over. Those who do no more than act as if they're on track with these innovations are trying to bring the edge to the core, where it can easily be smothered by institutionalized traditions and processes, the firm's essential inertia. Leaders must think hard about these dynamics, see the shifts taking place in their markets, and decide which platforms to develop for a future with the promise of new opportunities. Sometime this decade, the wheat and the chaff will be separated, the winners and the laggards easier to identify. A strong positioning program, in addition to an unambiguous long-term strategy, is critical to the future of successful firms. Multiple systems and platforms will need to be identified, developed, and adjusted. Old platforms will need to be transitioned out, converted, or shrunken to make space for the maturing edge systems and processes. The real power of the new ideas taking shape will be shown by how much muscle they provide us for escaping the old ideas that will be left behind as the Big Shift continues.

In their white paper called *The Big Shift: Why It Matters*, HBD discuss the intensified competitive pressures that firms have experienced over recent decades. Returns on assets for U.S. firms have steadily eroded, falling to almost one-quarter of 1965 levels. Big companies are losing their leadership positions at a higher rate, and their replacements at the top occupy increasingly precarious positions. Customer and client disloyalty has increased their power, creating more uncertainty and instability. The digital infrastructure has seen massive gains in price/performance capability as increases in computing, data storage, and bandwidth drive an adoption rate that is multiple times faster than that of previous infrastructures. These factors will continue to put performance pressure on all parts of the

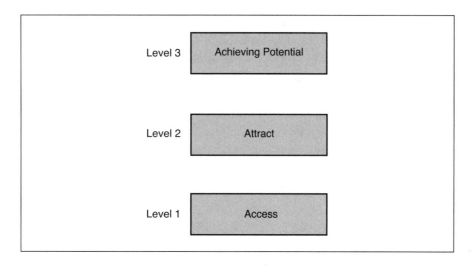

Figure 1.1 The three levels of the pull platform describe our mobilization in the new era. "Access" means reaching out; "attract" denotes connecting with the resources we need; "potential" represents how this process will help us meet our individual aspirations and goal. (Adapted from the writings of Hagel, Brown & Davison of DCE)

economy, potentially maintaining the downward trend in overall performance. This dynamic demands a shift from scalable efficiency to scalable learning. Scalable learning requires that firms find ways to unleash the creative potential of their entire workforce, and partner with firms interested in doing the same. It requires the pursuit of knowledge flows, as opposed to stocks of knowledge. As the world speeds up, stocks of knowledge depreciate at a faster rate. Product life cycles shorten dramatically, and new learning demands appear as soon as the current demand has been met. Participating in and benefiting from flows require more focus on "know how" than on "know what." Taking knowledge from a source without contributing knowledge will cause takers to be marginalized. Firms need to find and create new knowledge flow networks and economic webs that will reduce risk while enhancing learning and creating value.

Making these connections is the first order of business for making progress through the growing power of "pull." Pull platforms (Figure 1.1) help us make more flexible connections with people and resources in order to maximize our performance potential.

Access is defined as the ability to find, learn about, and connect with resources as needed to fill unanticipated needs. In the Big Shift, this capability becomes increasingly central to our survival and a prerequisite for our success, according to HBD. The world is moving from top-down, hierarchical push techniques to bottom-up, collaborative approaches emphasizing learning over efficiency and talent over routine organizational processes.

Search engines and business networking tools such as LinkedIn represent basic examples of access tools. When organized correctly, these tools aggregate resources across many thousands or even millions of people. The second level of pull, attract, is a more serendipitous process than searching and making deliberate connections. The overall landscape of social networks represents a growing opportunity to shape serendipity, increasing the probability and quality of chance encounters that offer people and resources you actually didn't know you were looking for. The third level of pull is achieving our potential, the ability to capture the insights and performance we need in order to move faster and learn faster by working with others. Moving up this collaboration curve requires broader and deeper commitments than those associated only with individual projects.

Central to reversing the decrease in performance and returns is the building of the plan your firm needs to harness the power of these pull dynamics. It starts with paying attention to individual catalysts in your organization, then proceeds with the steady, deliberate construction of a new platform to expand from nascent ideas to strong positioning for the firm, as the Big Shift continues to unfold. Expectations that this disruption will end soon should be discounted. The quick arrival at a new resting point, allowing for a stable business environment, is unlikely. We have entered a lengthy era of instability that requires our greatest skills to convert threats into opportunities, and edge ideas into core components.

Although various aspects of these trends and potential solutions apply to the design profession, also think about how they affect the markets and clients you serve. What pressures can your firm help them address through design, innovation, and improved project control and delivery? What decisions do you need to make to meet their emerging demands with more powerful tools and approaches to problem solving? Answers developed through a new lens will be required to meet the complex challenges of today and those just around the bend.

THE FOURTH TURNING

Also high on the list of thinkers speaking to us as we enter this unfamiliar terrain is a duo of historian-writers, William Strauss and Neil Howe, who have authored a series of seminal books relating to the cyclical nature of generational experiences and influences. Within a number of their books, *Generations: The History of America's Future, 1584–2069* (1991), *Gen X: Abort. Retry, Ignore, Fail?* (1993), *The Fourth Turning: An American Prophecy* (1997), and *Millennials Rising: The Next Generation* (2000), they have defined, posited, and captured a series of prescient events and cycles that all professionals and business leaders should become familiar with. Strauss and Howe believe that history is marked by 80- to 100-year cycles that match the lifespan of most human beings. These cycles consist of generations of 20 to 25 years that show remarkable consistency over history. Of course, not everyone in every generation acts alike, but we are shaped by our joint experiences and the forces of the time period in question. According to Strauss and Howe:

> Turnings last about 20 years and always arrive in the same order. Four of them make up the cycle of history, which is about the length of a human life. The first turning is a High, a period of confident expansion as a new order becomes established after the old has been dismantled. Next comes an Awakening, a time of rebellion against the now-established order, when spiritual exploration becomes the norm. Then comes an Unraveling, an increasingly troubled era of strong individualism that surmounts increasingly fragmented institutions. Last comes the Fourth Turning, and era of upheaval, a crisis in which society defines its very nature and purpose.

Looking at recent American history, our High began in 1946 with the victory in World War II. Dutiful sacrifice was made, and energy turned towards prosperity, solidarity, and stability. Our second turning, the Awakening, began in 1964, when institutions were challenged, and the quest for the greater meaning of things took hold. The fabric of American life that was constructed in the joyous postwar period was torn apart. This Awakening lasted until 1984, and the Baby Boomers became Yuppies. Thus began the Unraveling, even with the relative peace and prosperity of the times. However, what was developing underneath the good life was cultural wars, dramatic technological changes, and increased debt burdens that most never took the time to focus on, much less fix. According to the authors, the attacks of 9/11 marked the end of the Unraveling, and the beginning of the Crisis, the Fourth Turning. This would portend another 10 or more years of this crisis period before returning to the High of a first turning.

Along with the generational cycles, Strauss and Howe describe four dominant archetypes that dominate each generational phase. A summary of those archetypes and phases follows (Table 1-1); the generational descriptions are summarized in Table 1-2.

As the Baby Boomer Prophets enter their elderhood during this crisis period, pragmatic Nomads replace them as their midlife responsibilities to society grow. They portend a more conservative, tougher resolve to defend society, while safeguarding the interests of the young. This is in direct contrast to their early childhood experience of being underprotected by their indulged parents. This more hardened Generation X is inheriting a

TABLE 1-1: Archetypes and Phases of Life

Archetype	Childhood	Young Adulthood	Midlife	Elderhood
Prophet	Spoiled (First Turning)	Self-important (Second Turning)	Disapproving (Third Turning)	Futurist, imaginative (Fourth Turning)
Nomad	Free to roam, on their own (Second Turning)	At odds, independent (Third Turning)	Pragmatic (Fourth Turning)	Tired, traditional, guarded (First Turning)
Hero	Kept from harm (Third Turning)	Team player, faces obstacles (Fourth Turning)	Arrogant (First Turning)	Full of activity (Second Turning)
Artist	Protected, smothered (Fourth Turning)	Traditionalist (First Turning)	Knowledgeable but indecisive (Second Turning)	Overly sensitive, feeler (Third Turning)

(Adapted from *The Fourth Turning*, Strauss & Howe, 1997)

world where the simple imperative is: "Society must prevail." Given the range and depth of the current crises—environmental, fiscal, international, governmental—there will be an increased need for public consensus, aggressive approaches by ruling institutions (think of the Federal Reserve's actions), and personal sacrifice, to find our way through.

TABLE 1-2: Generational Turnings

	First Turning	Second Turning	Third Turning	Fourth Turning
Description	A high-mood era of supporting institutions and shooting down the individual, when a new community order develops and the old values are left behind.	Turmoil in relation to spirituality, when the old order is attacked by a new set of beliefs.	A time of social negativity as individuals take hold and institutions weaken, when the old social order crumbles and the new takes root.	A time of crisis when material and worldly views are weakened, and the new social order demands the replacement of the old.
Generational alignment	Older Prophets disappear, Nomads enter elderhood, Heroes enter midlife, Artists enter young adulthood—and a new generation of Prophets is born.	Older Nomads disappear, Heroes enter elderhood, Artists enter midlife, Prophets enter young adulthood—and a new generation of child Nomads is born.	Older Heroes disappear, Artists enter elderhood, Prophets enter midlife, Nomads enter young adulthood—and a new generation of child Heroes is born.	Older Artists disappear, Prophets enter elderhood, Nomads enter midlife, Heroes enter young adulthood—and a new generation of child Artists is born.

(Adapted from *The Fourth Turning*, Strauss & Howe, 1997)

As represented in an August 2009 *New York Times* article by Nicolai Ouroussoff, by the mid-1960s, the Modernist dream was in ruins, along with the belief that architecture could act as an agent of positive social change. Failed urban housing projects, government buildings without a soul, and sterile concrete plazas left the world of architecture in crisis. The argument could be made that the economic tailspin of the past few years will help architecture by putting an end to the gaudy boom of residential towers. Rents will fall, allowing a younger generation, creative and hungry, to begin a new cycle of more purposeful, human-scaled design. Who knows which direction this crisis will push/pull us in?

What is certain, however, is the importance of comprehending the generational cycles that regularly appear and, in their own way, allow us to ultimately move forward. It may not make a big difference whether this new crisis period is now 10 years along, or only began with the market turmoil in 2008. What does matter is that we take the time to view the world through this cyclical lens in order to better understand how society is likely to behave as the eras march ahead. For firms awaiting the return to normal, for those frozen with uncertainty or fear, it's time to thaw and begin to act. For those who grasp the opportunities presented by each cycle of life and civilization, it's time to design your firm's place in the spectrum of solutions that will get us through the fire.

PRAGMATISM

A third element of this funnel into the future is the philosophy of pragmatism as a response to the seeking of truth. Originally developed by Charles S. Peirce, America's original logician, pragmatism's essential maxim is that the process of inquiry results in the product called belief, certainty, knowledge, or truth. Peirce was a contemporary of William James, America's first great philosopher/psychologist, whose version of the pragmatic theory says that beliefs are not true until they have been made true by verification. James believed propositions become true over the long term through proving their utility in a person's specific situation. A period of crisis such as ours today is likely to draw out attempts to determine the absolute truth about our situation and the problems that define it. However, as seen throughout history, truth is relative to the times and to the knowledge an era has gained through science and other methods. The point is that there are going to be new forces in play, as our Fourth Turning plays out. The upcoming generation will be seeking to solve problems in a more practical and realistic fashion, and judgments of the quality of the outcomes will be primarily based on what worked, not on what might have worked better under different conditions. This phenomenon tightens the gap between seeking an ultimate truth and accepting practical decisions made on a more expedient basis. This expediency will affect society as a whole, and the design industry will also adjust to it. Practicality will become paramount to project owners who, with increasingly scarce and prized resources, will require increased assurance—and proof—that the direction, intent, and consequences of a project will be fulfilled as planned. This will lead to much greater scrutiny of the systems, methods, and tools employed in the achievement of those goals. Finally, that particular reality will lead to even stiffer competition among all firms for the work that becomes available.

THE EFFECTS OF SUSTAINABILITY

When design firms need to discuss sustainability with clients, what are the elements on the client side of the fence that are paramount to the management of the companies and institutions we rely on for adopting our initiatives? The reality is that top CEOs and management thought leaders are already way ahead on the curve. It's no longer a theoretical conversation. These leaders are thinking in concrete terms that are changing the practice of management and the cultures and habits that have gone unchallenged for decades. The following summary of these effects is drawn from a Fall 2009 *MIT Sloan Management Review* article, "8 Reasons (You Never Thought Of) That Sustainability Will Change Management," by Michael S. Hopkins, the first in a series that will move beyond the high-level implications into the details. The eight trends captured in this first report are as follows:

- Planning: Companies are being pushed by consumers, governments, labor, and a host of other forces to make sustainability a top priority on their strategy agenda.
- Productivity: Bottom-line benefits from energy savings and resource efficiencies get the attention of managers, but even greater efficiencies can be gained through labor productivity. Strategies include workplace design based on sustainability principles that can yield an average of 16% greater labor efficiency, far outpacing the energy savings alone.
- Reputation: Sustainability is a proxy for management quality. Rigor and thought leadership on sustainability confers positive connotations on other aspects such as finance, marketing, and technical quality.
- Strategy: Sustainability forces managers to look at their organizations from a higher vantage point, and what they can learn is surprising. At Coca-Cola, the search for embedded carbon in the value chain

led to the discovery of other waste in the system. When executives "connect the dots" this way, it's easier to see the entire ecosystem of the organization and address high-leverage issues that change numerous results throughout the system.

- Innovation: Sustainability challenges are unusually interdisciplinary, requiring greater collaboration across silos and business sector boundaries. Creating new and different conversations among previously unfamiliar groups leads to bursts of options that hadn't been considered, enriching the playing field for all participants.

- Coordination: With sustainability being a complex and systems-oriented problem, it requires coordination and collaboration across fiefdoms and geographic regions. Tremendous gains are seen in integration and communication, forcing companies to learn a different way of working.

- Partnering: Many corporate leaders have greater fear about risk, and their ability to assess risk is low. Organizations can gain advantage in the marketplace if they engender trust through their policies and practices. Being as transparent as possible will work to close the trust gap, and this will include new ways of tracking and measuring performance, especially in the financial arena.

- Advantage: Not unlike the early days of the Internet explosion, early movers on sustainability opportunities will accrue a strong advantage over competitors. And with sustainability holding enough sway to induce fairly sudden and dramatic changes within industries, executives are looking to leap ahead now in order to stay in front of the pack.

With the design industry squarely at the center of the sustainability movement, there's much to indicate a strong positive boost as this groundswell continues to grow. The current instability and uncertainty offer designers a unique opportunity to reach deeper into client industries' inner workings when developing solutions. Industry leadership is already there, and they're seeking the next set of ideas about how to go much further, much faster.

The implications of these generational cycles, world financial shifts, sustainability efforts, and emerging philosophies are not only significant for determining firm positioning, they also inform firm leaders regarding firm culture and recruiting strategies. We have entered an epoch for which we have no real comparison or point of reference. The reality for design firms is a picture of contrasts: As an industry designated to solve problems and advance the culture, we are faced with constraints that cut the underpinnings of progress to the core. New ideas simply aren't enough at this juncture in time. Ideas need to be quickly converted into actionable solutions that make a difference for clients and industries struggling to survive. More than ever before, this situation requires firms to walk in the shoes of their clients and understand the challenges of their markets in order to deliver the necessary value potential. These aren't goals that are easily achieved. They require substantially more determination and creativity than have previously been required to work through a classic "inventory-driven" downturn. The necessary skills and approaches can be discovered and developed through a strong positioning strategy, and the needs have never been greater, as we enter into the ultimate resolution of the Big Shift.

Firms need to understand that their previous methods of positioning, marketing, planning, and delivering projects are now undergoing substantive, lasting change. This isn't simply a function of increased competition for jobs that once were more easily winnable. This isn't only a matter of sprucing up the website, and redesigning the traditional marketing materials. An entirely new way of thinking and working is coming about.

Most firms have been hit squarely between the eyes by the severity of revenue loss over the past few years. The following story provides a glimpse of what it's been like for one firm in the South.

CASE STUDY: KPS GROUP, BIRMINGHAM, ALABAMA

THE GREAT RECESSION STRIKES

Looking back with the wisdom of experience, it seemed like the canary in the coal mine to Gray Plosser, FAIA, LEED AP, when the dynamics of late 2007 and early 2008 came into stark focus. As President of KPS Group, headquartered in Birmingham, Alabama, with a branch office in Atlanta, Georgia, he began to realize that their healthy backlog was disappearing faster than they could comprehend, almost 60 percent by the end of the first quarter of 2008. That shockingly rapid decline ultimately resulted in a 23 percent reduction of revenues from the previous year. Looking at those events with the clear eyes of 20/20 vision, Gray says he and his firm practiced artful denial in the face of the devastating loss of business. "We waited too long to get serious about changing our financial model to match the new revenue stream."

By late 2008, it was clear to him and his partners that fundamental macroeconomic issues were involved. As 2009 dawned, the firm finally began to see the situation as an opportunity, not a disaster.

By early 2009, there was a comprehensive cost reduction effort under way, including a 10 percent layoff, and the realization that keeping your head down to let the storm blow over wasn't a viable strategy. They began to make fundamental changes in their business development process, looking at where the dollars were and how they could match those sources with their expertise. "We knew by then we needed to enhance our positioning and our brand, acquire new skills, technology and know-how in order to re-capture the kind of competitive advantage we had enjoyed for many years." So, they got to work on just that.

KPS revamped its business development process while redesigning their project management and administrative functions, beginning with new hardware and software. Though historically committed to sustainable design, the firm focused on enhancing its brand message while achieving LEED accreditation for 100 percent of its professional staff. As Gray puts it, "We had a culture of being assertive in terms of getting business in the previous cycles. We now emphasize the expertise of our very talented staff as a highly skilled resource for our clients and promote service quality by being more attentive and responsive. We are not just a set of disciplines or capabilities." As a 48-year-old firm with a staff of 45 today, KPS Group offers architecture, interior design, landscape architecture, planning, and urban design as their core services.

Another issue that came into focus during this period was firm-wide productivity. KPS turned to fellow Global Design Alliance member CADFORCE, the Los Angeles–based company that provides CAD support services, construction document production, and BIM support services to firms around the world. KPS had won a large commission for additions and renovations to the Birmingham Airport terminal building and looked to CADFORCE to help migrate to Revit and avoid staffing up. CADFORCE provided a Revit PM to manage the overall transition, including weekly videoconferences to measure their success after the initial on-site visits. They helped KPS train a project team on the airport project, and through their outsourcing program built an 80 percent design development model. Additional design support and monitoring will continue towards a 60 percent CD appraisal in the spring of 2010. As Gray puts it, "This type of outside support allowed us the freedom we needed to focus on our markets and the major shifts that were occurring while implementing BIM on this significant project."

In addition to the external support, KPS made several critical hires, and began looking more closely at M&A opportunities to bolster future prospects. They looked inward and saw knowledge areas they possessed but weren't capitalizing on. From these realizations came a plan to repackage their knowledge and skills to penetrate their markets deeper, vertically. By the middle of 2009, with the Birmingham Airport contract in place, stability began to seem feasible again. "We surely got hit early, but it turned out to be a bit of an advantage," according to Gray. "The tailwind provided by the airport project came when everyone else was just realizing what a tough climb this recession was going to be."

And there are still many challenges remaining. With the Atlanta market being highly developer driven, that office has been hit hard. Gray is optimistic, but not without some trepidation. He has some fear for the firm and for the industry in general, saying, "This will be an exciting time, but not at all easy. There's going to be more pain and blood on the floor before it's all said and done. Our industry still has too much capacity and isn't efficient enough to close the gaps that exist with the amount of work that's likely to come along. The real question we all have to face is 'How do we make ourselves more valuable to the clients and markets, and society as a whole?'"

As soon as he poses the question, he proposes an answer. He thinks the greatest costs, and therefore the greatest opportunities, lie in the life cycles of facilities. He claims that the entire AEC industry needs to move from a transaction base to a service base, learning how to apply its skills to the life cycles of facilities, not just to the scope of designing and erecting the structure. "It's like we've been practicing as an obstetrician, and what we really need to do is think and practice approximating an internist."

The KPS Group experience is likely familiar to many thousands of firm leaders. During periods of significant upheaval, we tend to try to wait it out, hoping for a reasonably quick return to what was normal. But firm leaders who can subscribe to at least some of the precepts of *The Fourth Turning* and edge/core thinking will find that their positioning perspectives will be sharpened, and they'll have a chance to move ahead of the competitive curve when it comes to firm development for the new era.

CHAPTER 2

POSITIONING

POSITIONING DEFINED

The new economic and social realities unfolding around us demand that every firm seeking success in the post-boom era reimagine, redefine, and reenergize their position in the marketplace. Positioning is the concept and tool needed to achieve this outcome, and while its history is fairly recent, its power is substantial. No longer is high-level strategy enough to allow us to navigate through the land mines and booby traps of economic conditions. Future strategic advantage will come from a firm's commitment to a dynamic and growing positioning strategy that brings their 10–15 year strategic plan into focus. Changes to positioning will be demanded much more frequently than in the past. New technologies, new competitors, new client needs, and the shifting sands of economic stability will require firms to react more quickly and more boldly. Regardless of how many firms survive or fail, or how many designers are ultimately employed by the profession, clients and markets will still need the work to be performed. The real questions are: "What will change about the client needs?" and "What will it take to be one of the firms that thrive in the new era?" This era of change will likely last another decade, at which point it may settle into a somewhat more predictable "normalcy." Yet even that expectation is on the table for review, so best not plan for it anytime down the road.

So what is positioning? Positioning is the process that firms utilize to create a clear and compelling identity, image, and reputation in the minds of their target market. Secondarily, these same positive images should be conveyed to other professionals: other designers, partners, professional associations, academic communities, and the like. Positioning began as the turf of product marketers only, and remained that way for decades. Over the past two decades, design firms have joined the ranks of businesses, professional services firms, and others that recognize the value of planning for the long term. During this time, strategic planning became a mainstay for many in the industry, and annual marketing planning is perceived as a valuable exercise. Architects and engineers alike have learned that business plans are also necessary. More attention has been paid to websites, logos, and enough branding identity to qualify as "checked off." However, during this period, positioning has largely lagged behind, overshadowed by strategic planning—the "big process" that firms use to shape the future to their vision.

Part of the shift that's occurring is that positioning now needs to permeate the entire firm—every staff member, every function—in order for it to be competitively successful. Midlevel staff who contribute to the Life at HOK blog are positioning agents for that firm. IT support personnel who are seeking out the best tools to build a firm-wide integrated database are part of the positioning solution. Positioning has evolved to include a much larger purview and meaning than previously. But before we explore that aspect further, we should pay homage to some classic positioning examples.

Walk into any large, modern grocery store and you can easily observe positioning in action. In fact, if you're a regular visitor to the same store, you have been trained by both the owners of the chain and their suppliers and vendors as you make your way down the aisles. If the coffee isn't in the same place it's always been, the world seems a bit out of whack for a few moments. If the end-of-aisle displays have been rearranged for a holiday or a special event, you may have to stop and think where the bread is located, since you always pick up your English muffins at the end of the aisle, *right here*. From grocery store items to the placement of stand-alone drugstores at major intersections, the world has become a constant struggle for positioning to win the battle for the consumer. Take the process another step further, and branding takes over. Major advertised brands demand that their products be placed at eye level in the grocery store, where they are the easiest to see and grab off the shelf. Look up, and you might find the more exotic versions of the product; look down, and you need to stoop to save that 40 cents on the chain's private label.

Along this journey, the term "positioning" has also come into more common usage. *Positioning: The Battle for Your Mind*, by Al Ries and Jack Trout (1981), is considered the classic treatment of positioning, putting the term on the map. While their work was consumer-marketing oriented, the principles are as applicable to designers as they were to Avis, with its "We're #2, We Try Harder" slogan. The intention of positioning is to create an image or identity about a product, service, or firm in the minds of the target audience. It took a while for the evolutionary process to catch up, but today every design firm should be thinking about how to create and expand this type of market connection for the services they provide. However, that branding-oriented connection is just one piece of the puzzle, supported by the systems-oriented approach to positioning this book explores.

It's not difficult to identify a few firms in the design business that have succeeded in strongly positioning themselves with crystal-clear images. Gensler is the king of the workplace environment, and they support their claims by continually delivering leading designs and fresh research. Populous remains the worldwide leader in arenas, stadiums, and other large gathering spaces for humankind. For large, complex projects such as science centers and medical research facilities, HDR is a shining star. There are reasons for the reputation and recognition these firms attract, and it isn't only a matter of size.

Every firm needs to develop a positioning platform. The reason? If you don't, the market will provide an image for you, and that image is not likely to be powerful and positive. For many firms, the positioning effort is too often centered around the message "We'll do anything for anyone." This doesn't work, hasn't ever worked, and won't work in the future. Architects can be particularly drawn to the idea that positioning means a long list of market types, followed by a long list of services that clients can choose from. In reality, this only positions these providers as non-experts, and frequently results in mediocre assignments with marginal returns.

In an industry that is driven by individual project assignments, the diversity of "who you are" can be difficult to distill. Each time an economic wind blows, firms scramble to reinvent their focus, identity, and reason for being. Many may even have done their strategy work, and done it well. Then 2008 came along, and challenges that had been survived in 2006 or 2007 proceeded to wallop thousands of firms harder than ever imagined possible. This is not to say that dedication to a clear market focus would have kept every firm safe from this economic pain, but those who do the best during the bad times are less prone to abandoning markets in the effort to survive.

Whether for a newer firm or one celebrating 100 years in practice, a positioning platform is needed, and needs to be revisited and revived often. In the larger picture, a positioning plan performs two vital functions: It's a necessary bridge between the strategic plan and the short-term operating environment, and it's a tool that fosters stronger focus on the individual components of an evolving image and identity. Ultimately, firms that have strong positions in their chosen markets act like magnets for new work. They don't scramble as often to survive, and they aren't often distracted by too many new opportunities that would dilute the image they have built, or divert important resources from long-term goals. A positioning plan encourages the development of medium-range programs that support your strategy and inform your operating environment. It teaches staff a more systematic process for making decisions that relate to marketing and image building. And in a world that can often present an overabundance of options, it's useful for establishing the rules and guidelines necessary for putting out a consistent and well-integrated message.

Not every organization can reach the ultimate goal of being number one in their market. Rather than lamenting that fact, each product or service provider needs to be successful at carving out a version of being number one. Taking another look at Avis's "#2," it's clear that their long-term goal was to be number one at remaining number two, behind Hertz. This created an environment where they spent a lot of time and energy protecting their flanks, rather than attempting to occupy the top position. They cared more about what National, Budget, and Dollar were doing than anything else. Executed correctly, this approach can work well, galvanizing the troops, endearing the brand to the hearts of travelers, and earning good financial returns.

The Strategy-Task Gap

Without a positioning plan in place, firms often bounce around among client service issues, "go/no go" decisions, and various forms of firefighting, while attempting to make small improvements to key internal functions. And while a solid strategic plan can buoy an organization's view of tomorrow, the process of actually getting there can be quite frustrating. The experience of many firms is that the creation of good strategy quickly degenerates into the assignment of tasks that too closely resemble what the firm was already doing. The loftier vision of purpose and achievement gets pulled down by the gravitational force of day-to-day work, and the best strategies can't be realized. Positioning work, when done correctly, builds many logical connections between the elements of strategy and the tasks required to bring about real change. The chart in Figure 2.1 depicts the placement of positioning that provides the logic and connectivity required to implement a strategic vision.

Positioning work fills the gap between strategy and these tasks in a way that creates a highly visible, tangible set of components that need to be developed and arranged, to meet strategic goals and visions. So, while great

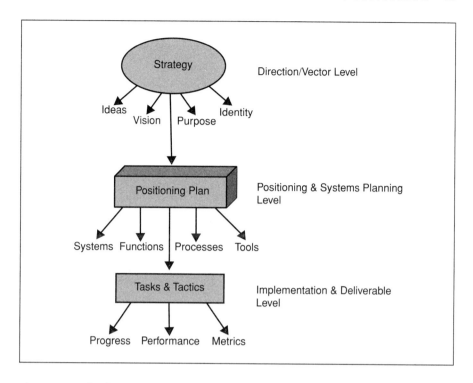

Figure 2.1   The firm's positioning plan connects strategy to everyday tasks and operations. It provides a modular systems view of the firm's progress, allowing for strategic alignment of important functions and processes. (*Source:* SPARKS, The Center for Strategic Planning)

strategy may contain as few as two or three well-defined ideas, all pulling in same direction, the positioning platform provides the connectivity—the numerous key elements that must be developed, strengthened, or adjusted in order for the firm to realize its destiny.

In this regard, this book builds on the common usage of the term "positioning," giving it much greater importance, depth, and purpose. It clarifies the implications of strategy, and guides the incremental efforts of the leaders and staff. It provides greater context for the relational aspects of firm development, including the traditional externally oriented positioning within a marketplace or with competitors. To use a driving analogy, it fills the gap between the map of U.S. interstates and the local street map by providing the map of the state itself.

THE POSITIONING PLATFORM FOR DESIGN FIRMS

The positioning platform is designed to organize many of the key aspects a firm needs to manage in order to achieve an ultimate strategic goal. It also

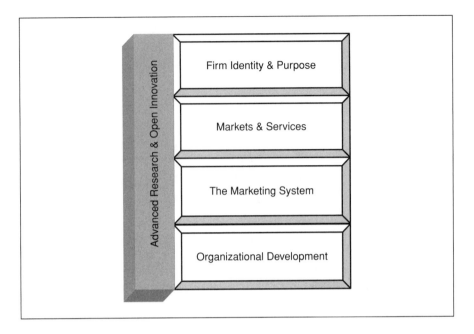

Figure 2.2 The Positioning Platform represents the systemic connections among key elements and functions that every firm needs to develop. Each portion of the platform contains numerous ingredients that require development in order to fulfill a positioning strategy. (*Source:* SPARKS, The Center for Strategic Planning)

creates the bridge between strategy and tasks, as previously noted. In the big picture, the positioning platform consists of five planks, as depicted in Figure 2.2.

Within each of the five planks, there are many elements that define the whole. There are seven for each plank, and the resulting 35 elements follow in Table 2-1.

These 35 elements form a broad swath of the "what" of the positioning topic. Before describing the "how," further definition of the broad elements is in order. Consider these snippets as a warmup to the greater depth of discussion in the next five chapters.

Firm Identity

Purpose: Successful firms have a purpose for their existence. This purpose transcends talent or any particular project, and creates the philosophical umbrella under which the firm operates. Purposeful firms realize that their future needs a guiding hand. Purpose can be discovered through the original passions of the founding leadership, or updated by the emerging needs of society. Purpose is best expressed when presented through the lens of

TABLE 2-1: The Positioning Platform

Firm Identity & Purpose	Markets & Services	The Marketing System	Organizational Development	Advanced Research & Open Innovation
Purpose	Design	Image	Leadership	Technical & design research
Operating model	Knowledge	Visibility	Efficiency	Sustainability
Vision	Skills	Reputation	Collaboration	Application development and integration
Strategy	Focus	Packaging	Processes and systems	Thought leadership
Commitment	Value and pricing	Recognition	Roles and responsibilities	Macro-collaboration
Expertise	Teaming	Business development	Capabilities	Open innovation
Structure	Geography	Networks	Infrastructure	Systems development

the community or market being served. An example of this might be: "Our firm is committed to providing the hospitality industry with the finest facilities and environments we can envision together. This commitment results in guest experiences, service, and comfort that define industry standards and help our clients achieve their greatest dreams." This statement of purpose is clearly more compelling than "on-time, on budget, with excellent quality," which only tends to commoditize the design industry's services.

A firm's purpose is larger than the next proposal, and more focused than the next announcement of a project that will divert your resources from your core markets. A clear statement of purpose not only establishes the goal, it also impresses the staff with the seriousness of the quest, and directs their thinking and efforts to that particular ambition.

Operating Model: Firm identity requires the selection of an operating model to ensure cohesive functioning that supports the firm's purpose and defines the parameters of how it will conduct its practice and business. Amazon versus Barnes & Noble is a neoclassic example of the clash between operating models, and the implications are clear. Both endeavor to sell books, but to achieve that goal, they offer customers markedly different experiences. Amazon tilts towards value and efficiency, while B&N satisfies the traditionalist's need for browsing within an environment for readers.

The SPARKS Framework Assessment is a tool that allows firms to look at their current and desired future operating models, and make informed, integrated choices. This assessment tool is included in the appendix of this book.

Vision: Vision, while related to the firm's purpose, is more specific to the particular aspects of a market the firm wishes to serve. To expand on the hospitality industry example, the vision may lean on the firm's previous experience with the design of coastal resorts. A resulting vision statement might be: "To provide design services that achieve the optimal integration of the guest's land and sea experiences while visiting our client's properties." The vision statement begins to provide a tangible sense of what might be created, in addition to identifying the industry niche that the firm wishes to serve, as is done by the purpose statement.

Strategy: Strategy development is a process that contains the blank slates of purpose, operating model, and vision, and provides an intellectual format for creating the firm's essence and connecting it to the firm's daily activities. Strategy is itself a tool to establish focus, since a strategy that is all-inclusive for any markets, project types, or services isn't much of a strategy at all. The truest purpose for a strategy-building exercise is to define the direction (and destination) of the firm, and in doing so, to begin to understand the implications of that specific direction. If an airliner is taking off in New York and heading for London, there are different considerations than if the trip were to Boston. These considerations affect everyone connected to the endeavor, from the airline company executives to the pilots, attendants, city authorities, vendors, and the passengers themselves.

At minimum, strategy is the tool required to pull together the firm's "top line" view of what it is, why it exists, and where it's going. As mentioned earlier, if this activity devolves too much into the task-definition mode, attention to the strategic elements will be diluted. Planning teams can more readily leave a strategy session prepared to perform limited tasks (the bottom line) than to absorb and interpret the implications of strategy. It's largely for this reason that the positioning process exists: to provide the mid-level tools and processes needed to connect these two very different activities.

Commitment: Commitment is a soft word with a hard-edged meaning. It isn't included here to address an architect's or engineer's commitment to his or her profession. It's here to emphasize the need to commit to the creation and maintenance of a firm's identity, purpose, vision, and strategy. Many strategy sessions are held, and many of the results are ignored or overlooked when the bell rings to begin the next day. Commitment is also a function of the organizational development (OD) and leadership discussion, and, as with many of the words listed as key components of a particular plank, it applies across the platform. Obviously, a variety of important commitments are necessary when building and operating something as complex as a design firm. What may not be as obvious is the effect of a less-than-complete commitment to fully understanding and utilizing the tools available to create an organization that knows how to move mountains when necessary instead of driving around them.

Expertise: The topic of expertise also contains many cross-currents to elements such as market focus, knowledge, and efficiency. When a firm determines its purpose and drills down into the markets and the project types it chooses to serve and deliver, it then has the opportunity to develop a level of expertise that can lead the industry. This decision attracts the right talent, and the right talent will drill even deeper to achieve their individual career goals. In this context, the antonym of expertise is diversification. Some strategic diversification can be useful, especially when a firm is engaged in multiple markets that can have countercyclical characteristics. However, diversification for its own sake, or diversification undertaken out of fear of a market's demise, often indicates a weakness in the overall strategic fabric. Specialization that requires ever-greater levels of professional expertise within markets and project types will not be disappearing anytime soon, regardless of the state of the economy.

Structure: Structure is another way of saying locations, number, and types of offices and their geographic coverage. Many civil engineering firms are structured around a cluster model. Numerous firms decide to cover a state, or maybe just a section of a state, and never venture beyond those territories. Other firms see themselves as national or international presences, and through a combination of organic and merger/acquisition growth, give birth to new offices. Structure also implies the roles and capabilities of the locations involved. Is every office full-service? Are some locations mostly marketing fronts, with all the project operations handled in the home office? Are offices and/or their territories measured and managed the same way?

Given the economic turmoil of the past few years, some of these questions might seem moot or irrelevant. Yet moving in the reverse direction by shrinking a firm carries with it most of the same questions, as many have learned the hard way. An office that is closed under the stress of economic weakness may contain some talent and contacts that will disappear permanently. Conversely, a newer skeleton office may wind up with the healthiest clients, based on pure luck of the draw, making it more difficult and more expensive to provide those clients with the types of services and expertise they demand.

Determining a firm's structure in relation to both overall strategy and the economy is tricky business. What's required to make the best decisions in either a growth or cutback mode is a set of criteria that looks beyond the immediate, looping back to the direction in which the firm is committed to traveling.

Markets and Services

Design: The topic of design cuts across the entire positioning platform, and many firms consider it their number one service. However, the word alone can't begin to convey true meaning, so each firm needs to determine what design means to them and to their clients. Writers who use too many flowery words can dilute the ideas they're attempting to convey. Likewise, designers can over-design to meet their self-determined level of design requirements and lose the client's trust. From a service provider point of view, design needs to be strongly connected to the firm's purpose, role, and target client base. Once that is determined, the firm needs to staff itself with talent that understands and can deliver at that level. Design is a bit like monetary compensation. If I want to earn a steady wage and be guaranteed a modest cost of living increase, I should work for a large public institution. If I dream of bringing home a $500,000 bonus check someday, I'd best go to the edge of risk and reward and see who's out there.

Many firms seek to raise their design game, as a professional aspiration and/or as a competitive necessity. The difficulty arises when the firm's positioning doesn't agree with either of those needs, and the internal and external image of the firm comes under scrutiny. What's important is that the leadership make a decision—as painful or as exciting as the result might be—and maintain a well-integrated firm that satisfies and challenges the talent of their designers, while meeting or exceeding the needs of their clients. While such a balance may seem difficult to create, the real issue is that the topic isn't often dealt with head-on and with conviction.

Knowledge: Two types of knowledge are most relevant within the markets and services plank: One is the collection of knowledge on topics that are critical to the design industry, and therefore to the competitive positioning of the firm. These might include the usual suspects of green technology, sustainability, energy modeling, and the like. The other is knowledge of the markets the design firm serves. A firm that takes knowledge development seriously understands that their positioning capabilities are driven by knowing and learning whatever will best serve their target markets. If the firm's clients are truly the leaders in their industry, the opportunity to achieve something great is probably just around the corner. Consider the distinction between taking on a full-sized Panera Bread restaurant prototype versus a traditional Dunkin' Donuts design assignment. One is a more dynamic opportunity to create something special, and the other embodies the hope that you can convince the client to step up their game. A firm with vast knowledge and experience in retail and fast food will have the opportunity to bid and win both of these projects, whereas a lesser firm with just some general retail experience will be lucky to get their proposal read. Knowledge is power, and when it translates to a deep understanding of the challenges and opportunities faced by the leading clients within an industry, the design firm can become a sought-after resource. Other aspects of the knowledge question are explicit versus tacit, as will be discussed in Chapter 7.

Focus: The importance of focusing on specific markets (and project types) cannot be overstated when it comes to both the efficient and effective application of design services. And while this point is made in the preceding section on firm identity, the word is included here to emphasize the need to decide. Design firms that understand their markets deeply do so because of the decision to focus. When they make a presentation to win a job, it's about the client's world, not about the services the design firm can perform.

Value and Pricing: From an architect's perspective, offering value often means cutting back on the design effort. For an engineer, it may mean finding alternative systems that can do the job, but may not be as well made or operationally efficient. Or perhaps neither of those statements is actually related to value. Too often, the quest for value is a compromise related to dollars, and that shortchanges everyone involved. Successful positioning as a value-producing firm is much more creative and demanding than a simple cost-cutting exercise. Architects who are well positioned with a powerful client have the opportunity to define the thought process that results in creating value on the project. Too often, this opportunity lies fallow until the project is nearly under way, and the client is frantically looking for ways to save money.

Pricing, the setting of fees for services, is strongly related to a firm's positioning success or lack thereof. Understandably, firms are reluctant to cut fees even in the face of mounting competition and economic uncertainty. One aspect of this dynamic is the relationship to profitability, and one can argue that there is much more room to adjust fees when more attention is paid to internal efficiencies and operational systems. Under this construct, it is possible to reduce fees and increase profits, something firms should consider regardless of the current economic climate.

Teaming: Successful teaming with other professional services providers is a vital aspect of a design firm's success. While it may be difficult to find partners who are truly on the same page, the effort must be continuous. Many projects are conducted with arm's-length relationships, at best. Too many projects wind up with firms at odds with one another over technical, cost, or schedule problems. Architects have a unique opportunity to change the experience of teaming through the establishment of a more strategic relationship with the owners. Leaders and senior project managers need to invest more deeply in the early processes of working with owners to define the criteria for partner selections, and also need to make sure there is both philosophical and performance-related proof of what those firms have to offer. In addition to this owner-focused effort, firms need to independently nurture partnerships that can create synergies related to research, service branding, innovation, and joint programs to educate and influence specific markets. Firms need to identify goals that specify the nature and quality of the outcomes desired, and then need to build initiatives that establish their larger team as the best qualified to lead the client's most challenging projects.

Geography: A firm's geographic footprint and ultimate geographic reach are a key part of the positioning puzzle. Clearly, this aspect of a firm's identity cuts across all planks in the platform, and requires careful consideration, regardless of the business cycle. Many firms have expanded their reach through mergers and acquisitions over the past 10–20 years. Many of these ventures have worked well, but most have experienced unexpected difficulties, sometimes causing significant harm to the firms. Growth from a geographic perspective requires strict criteria in order to succeed. Sometimes what seems like a good working relationship is masking deeper issues that only get exposed once the merger is consummated. Leaders should spend more time considering safety nets when entertaining a significant M&A activity, and should find ways to look more closely at the motivations and assumptions of both sides.

Organic growth presents its own set of quandaries when it means expanding the firm's geographic reach using in-house resources. Unless an individual has "been there, done that" before, the firm needs to move carefully before assuming that he or she has the capabilities to start up an entire business operation in a new territory. Comfortable, long-term relationships can skip over the due diligence needed to design the best process for assessing potential and putting all the pieces in place. Chief among the issues are the individual's business development and management skills once he or she is away from the home office. Unless the firm is being taken to a new locale by a large and stable client who is demanding immediate local support, leaders should be putting in three times the effort and reducing expectations by 50 percent when it comes to opening new locations for their services.

The Marketing System

Image: A firm's positioning image can be a tricky aspect to change once it's been established over the years. If the firm is mostly local or covers a small regional area, it's likely that there's a comfortable view of the firm as established, reliable, and "doing good work." That image is often tied to the owners/partners who have nurtured key relationships and are considered part of the fabric of the communities they serve. Firms in this position aren't usually the ones that are motivated to break out with daring new ideas or deep, market-focused strategies. This image of stalwart service providers leaves these firms vulnerable to an erosion of fee leverage, and the threat of out-of-town market experts coming in to win the better projects in their traditional territory.

A narrower, yet stronger image emerges when a firm holds back from bidding on the vast array of work that becomes available within a reasonable distance. Visit their website, and you will likely find a stronger trend of project types for more substantial clients. Dig deeper, and you may well find the earmarks of a story that's developing as the firm adds more specialized talent to their roster.

Then look at the latest profile of a firm already known for being an industry leader. Even if their book of business has fallen off in recent years, they aren't abandoning their core commitments to markets and the role they play for clients. Original research is still being produced, new ideas still are in evidence on their blog and in their press releases, and significant clients are still ringing them up to discuss the future, if not specific project opportunities.

Image creation and management are critical parts of the marketing system, and require a keen, sober understanding of where the firm has been and who is competing for their share of the image pie. Yes, the world of image making has some limits. Consider a low-budget film that gains huge word-of-mouth support. It may move on to make millions, but the ticket buyers are only going to see that one film that night, that week, or that month. Clients have a similar limitation to how willing they are to expand their established beliefs when it comes to image. Put in the years of effort to build the one you want, and they will trust that image for a good long while. Leave the image making to the random chance of what others may or may not be saying about the firm, and it's likely that commoditization of your services and your brand will happen long before you realize it.

Visibility: Visibility is the generic process of getting the firm's name and work out into the mix of the marketplace. Whether it's for a traditional local firm, or for a high-flying international powerhouse, the process is essentially the same. Visibility relies on having stories to tell and information to share. Some firms can go 30 years before they think it's a good idea to hang a banner on the outside of a site under construction. Others won't miss any opportunity to expand their image and brand awareness through any means possible. For most firms, the right answer probably lies somewhere in between. It's important to overcome a few misconceptions when you begin to think about visibility within your positioning plan. First, there's the need to overcome a bit of self-consciousness about using a megaphone to announce your arrival, involvement, or contribution. The firm's staff, competitors, and future prospects all will notice, and all of that is a good thing. Second, it's hard to make a tactical mistake when you're putting the firm name further out into the realm of public relations. Press releases, sponsorships, and speaking engagements are all worthy approaches to achieving the goal, and each has little downside for the firm or the individual. Lastly, many leaders and marketers can make the mistake of talking too broadly about the firm. Clients want and need to hear specific stories about people, ideas, and the inside story of how the firm is putting the pieces together for a new initiative.

So, while visibility is certainly a broadcasting-oriented effort at one level, it also needs a voice speaking to others at a more personal level. Find that right combination of messages, and it will develop into a powerful tool that carries the firm's dynamics far along the path towards the future.

Packaging: A well-developed marketing system demands that a high priority be placed on the packaging of firm information, ideas, services, people, and knowledge. As in the perfume business, the product needs to carry its weight, but the packaging attracts the attention that often makes the sale possible. The right packaging and message about a mundane service you've always performed can shake up a client's perceptions. Invest in a four-page 8.5×11 white stock brochure written by two of your in-house experts—on a topic such as discovering unforeseen conditions through the application of the right technology—and your image will be enhanced a notch or two. Continue this type of output on a regular basis, say two or three times a year, and people will begin to believe you're seeking a leadership position in technology applications. Follow up with specific success stories, and the wet cement of potential will harden into a durable form that has changed the firm's image. Packaging is powerful.

Packaging people is also very powerful. Whose voice will transmit the newest ideas and possibilities that the firm is exploring? Who will lead the staff to the next pasture, where grass is greener and the firm's capabilities and ambitions can be best realized? Virtually every firm has that person, either already leading that charge, attempting to convince the other leaders that it's the way to go, or secretly looking for the opportunity to expand his or her aspirations to that next level. Although standing on a pedestal can feel a bit disorienting at first, a firm with no one legitimately placed on a pedestal degenerates into a place where there's no one to look up to.

Products created within a services environment are powerful. The list of services provided by most design firms is standard and uninspiring. Where is the unique twist on the description of how that service can be applied? Who is putting in the extra hours to turn the hidden, black-box processes of the firm into visible, more concrete products that clients can see and grasp? Which studios are collaborating to create the definitive version of the way the firm assesses a client's situation and needs, turning it into a tool that can educate those same clients about the firm's thought processes and skills?

Reputation: Reputation has a lot to do with starting smart and finishing strong. All complex endeavors have problems along the way. The best firms with the strongest reputations know how to get out of the blocks, and how to deliver the final outcomes. Some messiness in the middle can be forgiven when it's sandwiched between those two realities. Reputation can't be sought; it is earned. It tends to come in smaller units—more discreet than a press release, not as specific as a design award.

Reputation is the aroma of the meal that has been a long time under preparation. Smarter leaders also understand that there are a variety of vessels that get filled or emptied when it comes to reputation. Individuals might have a great and greatly deserved reputation, while the firm does not. Certain services and processes may receive praise, while others are silently tolerated as inferior or unworthy of comment. Take a plain piece of paper, draw up pictures of the firm's various vessels, and fill in the amounts that correlate to a clear measurement of "reputational" achievement. Take these visuals to the next staff meeting, and get reactions and alternative views. Then pick the two areas that are well below the line and get to work.

Recognition: Recognition is the bright and clear reflection of all the effort and results connected to the elements of image, visibility, and reputation. True recognition occurs when the firm's internal pedestal standing is replaced by the external world's decision to provide that higher perch. Firms and individuals that receive recognition from a community, a client, a market, or a professional association know the difference between a run-of-the-mill accolade and recognition of a special and unique achievement. True recognition doesn't simply happen; it's the result of a specific decision that has been developed and formed over a long period of time.

Most firms have some form of in-house recognition program, and this is an important element within the firm's culture and organizational development. The process of recognizing people and teams properly can actually take some practice. Specificity, fairness, timeliness, and the nature of the reward can at times be a vexing set of variables to navigate well. If this is so difficult with people you know, imagine how much more difficult it must be to achieve externally generated recognition that accurately hits the mark. The way to begin is to decide what the next five or ten years are meant to create. What higher-level role will you and/or the firm seek to occupy? Which client types are you best aligned with, to form teams to analyze the industry's biggest challenges?

In the end (and at the beginning), significant recognition can't be sought. It grows from the needs of individuals to achieve something of significance for the benefit of others. The best recognition is ultimately selfless, and that's a clue as to how to begin.

Education: Education is the process that funnels a firm's knowledge, capabilities, and ideas into a targeted area so it can be viewed, discussed, appreciated, and consumed. Within a healthy marketing system, the process of education is paramount, and operates within and outside the walls of the firm. The within part is fairly easy, yet seldom done well. Those who know, share, and those who need, listen and ask. All too frequently, however, this simple process is devoid of inspiration. It's a mundane transaction based on fairly dry facts and circumstances that leave any sense of discovery somewhere down the street. The question that results from this situation is: "If we can't excite those who are within our grasp, how will we ever inspire those who have no allegiance to us—the clients?"

Staff members need inspiration. They are hungry not just for the facts, but also for the possibilities, the reaching for the stars that can propel a career forward and answer the question, "Why did I ever decide to become a designer?" If a firm lacks an education program that not only conveys information but also challenges and inspires, it may be time to look into how it's done.

Clients are also hungry for a quality education. Is your firm leading the way when it comes to presentations at client industry conferences? Are principals scrambling to get ideas together that can paint a picture of the client world no one else has yet devised? Is the firm packaging its best skills and knowledge base (let's say it's BIM), and customizing three versions: one for clients who have zero experience with it, one for clients who are on the leading edge, and one for your team partners? Is the calendar filling up with occasions where these versions can be delivered, refined, and improved with feedback and new ideas?

Education is the marketing and positioning tool to end all searches for better tools. What counts is the commitment, the verve and contagiousness that go into the design of the material, and the ability to lead a group in exploration closer to the edge of possibility. Have you experienced that effect recently, either as a presenter or an attendee? Would those experiences begin to reposition your firm as a leading contender for the next strong projects that come along? The world may need to get along without another generic list of "Top Trends for the Next Ten Years" masquerading as true education. Teaching and educating should draw people in for a shared experience, and it's the only way to think when you want to connect with and influence an audience.

Business Development: Whether we're referring to the newest chief marketing officer or a classic "bird dog" behind the wheel on the way to the third state this week, all business needs development by someone. But the real question is: "Where does the development process need to begin?" Always beginning at the beginning can be just successful enough to keep a firm in business, but rarely enough to provide any significant breathing room. One large goal of the positioning process is to reduce the traditional business development time to as little as possible. Positioning is designed to bring opportunities to the door, where they can be welcomed in and offered a cup of coffee. Of course, the invisible escorts leading these new clients to the door are the 35 elements of positioning being presented here.

The outreach of the essential business development activity will always be needed. The difference will be that a firm that has done its positioning work will be treated like a long-lost relative who has money. Business development is so much easier when you're a known quantity, and one goal of the chief cold caller is never to make another call to a contact who knows nothing about the firm. What would it take for every possible prospect you can imagine to be on the receiving end of enough information, invitations, press releases, product descriptions, and project profiles that you'd never be considered a stranger again?

When the telecom business was struggling with creating networks that could deliver the promises of fiber optics, the constant bottleneck was that "last mile," getting from the local distribution hub to your house. With the design industry, it's actually the first mile that's the problem—driving to that meeting where you hope against hope that they'll remember your name in the hour it takes to get there.

Organizational Development

Learning: It may well be true that, besides the basic tenets of making money and servicing clients, every firm needs to be committed to learning. A learning environment bolsters project execution, enriches the staff, and develops the firm's reputation as a great place to work. Learning is both a formal and informal process. It requires disciplined thought and attention, and every role in the firm should have a set of learning (or teaching) responsibilities.

In many small and medium-sized firms, specialized capabilities are often the purview of only one or two individuals, and over time these staff members can be seen as "owning" their particular function. On the other side of the office, less experienced staff struggle with the normal array of design, technical, and standards decisions, not always sure where to go for help or not comfortable with approaching senior staff with problems. Additionally, there typically isn't a formalized periodic assessment process to take a snapshot of where strengths, weaknesses, and gaps exist.

Too often, new staff can be on board for many months before they're introduced to everyone, finally getting a clearer picture of who does what, who knows what, and so forth. Furthermore, when specialized knowledge and skills are thinly represented in an office, how does the firm safeguard against the loss of that valuable resource? Firms that allow this random and haphazard approach to developing key functions and staff will find themselves at a real competitive disadvantage. When younger staff leave what was originally a promising position, the underlying reason is often that they aren't learning enough, or that the organization makes it too difficult for them to access the right resources on a timely basis.

Is your firm promoting a learning environment to build achievement and career satisfaction? What processes are in place that all staff members can utilize to expand their understanding of new or complex topics?

Infrastructure: Infrastructure refers to the tools and systems used to support project operations, administration, human resources, marketing, and other key functions within the firm. Without a well-designed infrastructure, important information is lost or doesn't get shared. Beyond the technical IT aspects, the right infrastructure represents institutional memory and serves as a guide for work standards. It feeds the right information to the right people at the right time. It tracks activities and decisions, and eases the strain of tracking time spent and making billing summaries. From a marketing perspective, the right infrastructure streamlines proposal development, allows access to client history, and provides tools for analysis. Financially, the systems need to be linked in order to obtain an accurate picture of the firm's financial status and trend. When firms fail at the opportunities connected with infrastructure development, the reason isn't normally a lack of investment in software or hardware. For many firms, the issue is a lack of control and discipline, resulting in the random distribution of knowledge and processes throughout the organization. Individual principals and project managers may think the "official" system is too cumbersome, and develop their own methods on their PCs, making do as well as possible. When a particular studio sees its work as unique from the rest of the firm, it may develop a stand-alone, disconnected marketing system that makes the work of pulling together a firm-wide story that much more difficult.

A commitment to a unified, system-driven infrastructure is necessary for a firm to realize operational efficiencies and the sharing of information. Without such an approach, the firm's look and feel may depend on whom you're dealing with, eroding the firm's image and creating unnecessary work for already overburdened staff members.

Processes: The definition of and adherence to standard processes are critical to the firm's development of a smoothly functioning infrastructure. From an operations perspective, processes allow for greater efficiency, quality, and consistency. When everyone is free to invent his or her own methods for implementing a service, or ordering supplies, or conducting a staff appraisal, the results can be messy, at minimum. Autonomy and individuality are hallmarks of the design profession, but firms need to be clear that official processes should be developed and need to be followed. Once a firm decides "this is how we do it," the decision needn't stand as a bureaucratic roadblock. In fact, the best processes are those that can evolve, not those that are over-designed from the outset. Problem solving and the creation of better ways to do things should be a regular part of the process discussion in the firm. From a leader's perspective, the importance of absolute compliance with a defined process can vary depending on the topic, but the staff should clearly understand that the goal is to conduct as much business as possible within the steps and systems the firm has invested in.

Roles and Responsibilities: "Everyone markets, and everyone services the clients" could represent the essence of the beliefs of many firms, when it comes to roles and responsibilities. Simple, straightforward, and seemingly unassailable—but when everyone has the same job description, it can mean that no one is responsible for what goes wrong, or worse yet, for what gets ignored completely. In many firms, the only distinction between a partner and a senior project manager may be the fact of ownership. All too often, there is a laxness about deciding who's in charge of some important functions, and these get passed around like the proverbial hot potato when the mood strikes. The development of clear roles and responsibilities is vital to the maturing of the firm and its staff. Without such clarity, processes aren't developed, systems aren't built, and a substantial infrastructure remains a distant dream. Leaders who understand the importance of role clarity are looking at their people and functions in a systems view. They understand how easy it is for people to think they're doing the right thing, but wind up in a ditch. They see the importance of responsibility relationships between important functions, and they establish complementary roles so that the marketing director is legitimately aware of whether the operations director is successful. They define important initiatives as extensions of a person's role in the firm, and heighten expectations for a good outcome. They see critical gaps in the organization that need to be filled by an entirely new role or function, typically brought about by the demands of growth or perhaps the departure of key personnel. Have you taken the opportunity to review your firm's roles and responsibilities on a systemic basis? Are there recent events or changes that will allow an important role to be developed further, reassigned, or established from scratch? Which of the common complaints and frustrations from your staff might indicate that there's a misalignment of responsibilities needing to be investigated?

The efficiencies and increased organizational effectiveness that can be realized through a strong focus on roles and responsibilities are important lubricants for the firm's positioning effort, and need to be seen on the firm's dashboard with regularity.

Leadership: While there is no single, consistent, all-encompassing definition for the term "leadership," it does operate in two broad categories. The first is related to the person's position within a firm, normally conferred in concert with an appropriate title and at least a broad set of responsibilities. The second category is more skill-centric, recognizing those who, regardless of title or the permanence of certain responsibilities, display the qualities and traits of what the organization considers a leader to be. Leaders can be recognized from their visionary capabilities, their communication skills, their functional/technical expertise, or some combination of similar elements. Some in positions of leadership feel it is a burden—a somewhat unfortunate circumstance they neither sought nor know how to deal with. Others in official leadership roles see it as the ultimate opportunity to shape their corner of the world into a system functioning at the highest level, one that can take on great challenges and thwart all threats.

In the design industry, leadership can be an anointment based on ownership, and while this makes perfect sense, it too often results in ineffective management. Additional leadership posts are created as a firm grows, representing key functions and a variety of skill categories. The issue for the industry is that these positions are frequently seen as the end of the road: "I have arrived, I can now maintain my perch in whatever fashion I see fit, and my responsibilities are mostly to myself and the set of clients I serve." This type of thinking is not only a source of stagnation, but it can also be destructive to the healthy growth and exploration every firm needs.

The best leaders see their roles less as authority figures than as shapers of others who can benefit from their experience, perspective, and insights. Leaders see possibilities, organize these potential achievements into right-size portions, and seek out those who will take on the task of pursuing the end results.

Another way of viewing the leadership topic is to see the choices as transactional and transformational.[1] Transactional leaders oversee the groupings of tasks towards a specific completion point. Transformational leaders develop function, nourish people, and design systems so that the transactional work is accomplished with efficiency, accuracy, and the expected financial return. Execution is important, but leaders need to be focused on achieving development in addition to getting the work done.

Values: Values-based organizations establish a "third eye" for navigating the firm. Value systems are principles and beliefs that speak to the inner self of the individuals working for the firm, outlining the behaviors and viewpoints that should guide the conduct of their professional life, both within and outside the firm. Every value system needs to be refreshed periodically to ensure that it continues to provide meaningful guidance for the staff, and that it is applied with consistency and sincerity. Although many value systems develop organically and fairly randomly, care should be taken to shape the message of values into a thoughtful set of tenets that align not only with the beliefs of the firm's leaders, but also with societal and client norms and expectations. A value system statement can also provide a challenge to meet a higher standard, one that the firm may not yet be achieving.

Beyond stating specific values, such a belief system should be active, continuously seeking to find the weaknesses and holes in its interactions. From a positioning standpoint, a firm's value system needs to run parallel to the direction of the firm. If innovation is part of the firm's direction, then risk and failure need to be valued appropriately. If there is a dedication to a specific industry sector, such as the education sector, the firm's values should resonate with the underpinnings of that client type. Values are also a teaching opportunity, and leaders need to develop skills that allow for the discussion, presentation, and generation of stories relating to firm values. Without a strong, visible commitment, there is a risk of hollowness that can too easily influence other aspects of the firm's activities, potentially leading to a level of cynicism that can restrict organizational progress across the board.

Networks: The creation of networks and the inclusion of extra-organizational partners within the scope of a firm's development are critical to long-term success. Firms that are overly opportunistic will run from one new partner to another in the attempt to latch onto a new project. Firms that are clear about their strategy and positioning goals will carefully seek

---

[1] Burns, James M. *Leadership,* Harper & Row, 1978.

out partners that align with that direction and can technically support the needs of the projects they wish to pursue. Quite often, design firms are left to strategize in isolation, never feeling confident enough to invite key provider partners into the process. History is littered with the sour results of various alliances, joint ventures, and other contractual agreements that were intended to benefit all, and instead left many feeling shortchanged. This is often the result of the gap between firms in terms of strategy and tactics. When a firm is seeking to develop long-term partner relationships, they can easily be fooled by another firm that talks a good game but fades once real action or investment is required.

Unfortunately, most professionals interpret networking as simply another word for lead development. To be successful, firms need long-term collaborative networks, and in order for these to develop, there must be an alignment of the participating firms' philosophies, value systems, market knowledge, and client management skills. Successful positioning on a project-by-project basis will become increasingly difficult as more firms invest in powerful partnerships that are designed to transform project execution within an entire client market. These dynamics have been developing over the past two decades and will only accelerate as the new world order of economic realities pushes us further into the territory where only the strongest survive.

Advanced Research and Innovation

Technical and Design Research: The decision to engage in advanced research related to technical or design issues is a major commitment that not all firms will be able to step up to. For those that do, the best start is a focus on a particular project type or client type, in order to maintain contextual boundaries for the exploration process. This type of research can provide a terrific platform for macro-collaboration with resources that exist anywhere on the globe. A small internal research team can be identified, christened, and provided with a budget for developing their thinking and collecting data. From the start, the goals should include development of a useful application, and thought needs to be given as to how this application can be specified for use within ongoing project work. Teaming with universities, institutes, and professional thought leaders is the first order of business.

Sustainability: Sustainability is specified here, as opposed to saying simply "topical research," since it truly is the key to the future. Whether clients want energy modeling for net zero energy designs, climate-oriented siting, or building systems integration, every firm should be barreling ahead with a steep learning curve on this topic. If your firm can-not participate directly in research for sustainability, you ought to identify the best sources that speak the language of your markets and services, and devour everything available from their collective output. Use this infor-mation to conduct pre-proposal and pre-design sustainability reviews that force the project team to think beyond the RFP and beyond what's ac-ceptable in their previous experience. One issue with sustainability is that there's too much material out there for the team to read and consider every-thing. Make sure you're filtering the best information, so staff won't waste time on topics and ideas that aren't applicable or possible within your constraints.

Application Development and Integration: Except for the small hand-ful of firms that participate in pure research activities, firms need to gain something practical from their time and effort. Before committing to a larger team effort, make certain that you can reasonably identify the final product or result expected, and understand its applicability to your projects. In other words, make sure the activity has a good fit for your firm. If the research project is too nebulous, save that chair for someone ready to take on neb-ulous. If the team is simply going down an already known path and calling it research, it's a waste of your firm's time. Somewhere between those two conditions, you need to find a challenge you can contribute to, with an ex-pected outcome you can apply, and a result you can keep refining once it's off the good-idea page and into the drawings.

Thought Leadership: There are three choices in relation to thought leaders: (1) you are one, (2) you talk to one, or more, or (3) you read what they have to say on a weekly basis. It's time to catch up on books from the likes of Jason McLennan, who wrote *The Philosophy of Sustainable Design* (2004), and Janine Benyus, author of *Biomimicry: Innovation Inspired by Nature* (2002), as well as blog feeds and newsletters from a range of thinkers who regularly offer their findings and ideas to the public. That group should include someone like Tim Brown, CEO of IDEO, for broader-based design thinking that includes product design, process design, and aesthetics as well. Gather a collection of colleagues around the city, the country, or the world, and start a new group on LinkedIn to keep one another up to date and share new ideas between conference calls, which should be held every two months or so. Keep track of which thinkers have published articles, who has a book coming out, and where they are speaking. Communicate with these thinkers about the group's big ideas or most pressing questions. In other words, immerse yourself in the ideas of others who are anxious to understand the direction the world is moving in *as it's happening*, so you don't need to read about it ex post facto!

Macro-Collaboration: Collaboration has power and potential that most firms have yet to tap into. The "macro" part means that the collaboration is focused outside the firm, rather than internally or with project partners. Although internal collaboration is a function of teaming with other providers on a project, it typically doesn't demand depth of commitment or significant changes in longer-term thinking or behaviors. Deeper collaboration—practiced within an advanced research or innovation mode, for example—should be utilized by firms to create new templates for finding and developing strategic and positioning partners for the long haul. Setting the bar higher on the collaboration curve leads you from simply "cooperating well" to sharing discoveries and the developing ideas into meaningful applications that benefit clients and the market as a whole.

Open Innovation: Innovation is a great thing, but open innovation is even better. The image of a firm conducting secretive meetings and experiments to develop a new type of service may seem reasonable, but those images are now most often seen in the rearview mirror. Every firm needs to be willing to give away what they know. The best way to do that is to make it an investment in a collaborative group, using principles of open innovation as a guide.

Systems Development: Systems development can occur once leaders fully comprehend the price and inefficiency associated with piecemeal fixes to important processes and functions. When a firm can't easily manage (or even find) key information for developing an important proposal, it's likely the "system" in place isn't a system at all. When the marketing materials look and sound different from the website, which looks and sounds different from the last conference presentation, the only copy of which is on the conference speaker's computer, then the systems thinking of the firm needs some serious attention. Without reasonable systems integration, a firm cannot say it has a clear identity or a clear strategic direction. A strong positioning plan addresses the underlying aspect of systems development, allowing the firm to solidify its foundation and continue to build upward and outward while facing new challenges from competitors and clients alike.

CHAPTER 3

FIRM IDENTITY AND PURPOSE[1]

FIRM IDENTITY

Establishment of a clear and strong identity in the marketplace is the number one thing firms need to accomplish in order to succeed with their strategy and positioning efforts. Beyond the qualifications, experience, and talents associated with being a registered professional, the firm's identity choice provides the first piece of the overall positioning platform. While increasing numbers of firms realize the importance of this element, most are still lost in the identity fog and the operational complications that come with the lack of choice and follow-through.

Identity for a firm equates to the archetype or operating model that forms the foundation from which the firm functions. The SPARKS Framework Assessment (SFA), as seen in the appendix of this book, provides the basic tools that allow firm leaders to distinguish the basic identity that best suits their chosen role on the design stage. Table 3-1 lists these archetypes and the distinguishing driving force of each.

---

[1]Significant portions of this chapter were adapted from The American Institute of Architects, *The Architect's Handbook of Professional Practice*, 14th Edition, Joseph A. Demkin, Editor, John Wiley & Sons, 2008. The original writings are by Ellen Flynn-Heapes.

TABLE 3-1: Driving Forces Associated with Each Archetype

Archetypes	Distinctive Driving Force
Einstein	Cutting-Edge Innovation
Niche Expert	Perfecting the Specialty
Market Partner	Client Partnership
Community Leader	Community Connectivity
Orchestrator	Project Management Challenge
Builder	Cost/Quality Challenge

Can you answer the following questions? What are the firm's most deeply held values? What are its driving forces? How is it distinctive? How is it expert? What is its greatest value to the client? What does it hope to accomplish in the next 10 or 20 years? Would the best and most dedicated people accept an offer of employment from your firm? Since such professionals are ultimately volunteers, they have many opportunities from which to choose. They look closely at each firm's broader role in the industry, and pick a firm that's doing something they consider important. Companies need to have a clear understanding of their identity in order to attract, motivate, and retain outstanding people. This goes *double* for attracting the best clients.

"Tell us about your firm" is a request that frequently meets with the following set of answers. "We were established in 1909/1959/1999. We have 30/300/3000 people and 3/7/15 offices. We have this [laundry list] of services, and work in a wide variety [laundry list] of project types." Next in the formula is typically some perspective on the firm's approach to client service and ensuring quality. What's important here is that a description of basics won't have the impact needed to get a firm considered for something special: a project that can either put them on the map or keep them there.

The Source of Identity: The Driving Force

Although many firms operate expediently and reactively, most have a favorite place where they live—or at least aspire to. They have an array of values, but a single special one reigns supreme. The firm's supreme business value is called its driving force, and if your firm can capture it, you're on your way to building the right business model.

For example, the driving force of those who fit the *Orchestrator* model is a love of the logistics of a chess game. Project management, they believe, is the greatest challenge in the world, and the most worthwhile endeavor of all. They consider themselves an "elite cadre"—a SWAT team. As applied to their business design, we would see a very well-organized and planned firm, corporate in feel. Its top staff members are the best project managers. They have formal training curricula, and they make their highest profit on the most complex projects. All staff members understand what's really important.

Specific driving forces characterize each of the types in the framework assessment. They are shared, gut-level beliefs about what's most essential to accomplish together. More than any cultural value, such as integrity or collaboration, agreement upon these driving forces influences the success of the firm. Conflicts on this pivotal point, as discussed previously, can hamstring the firm, turning it into a bit player relegated to working on lower-quality projects.

When a company is probing for the deepest elements of its identity, there is often a common fearful protest: "You have to be flexible!" "You can't survive without having all these abilities!" "You have to keep looking for new opportunities!" And in fact, flexibility, openness, and responsiveness to clients are *always* required. But reactivity at a firm's core is predictive of a company that loses its way. Every firm must have a solid baseline of quality, efficiency, creativity, flexibility, openness, and client service in its work. The key is to keep your eye on where your real distinctive value is, and build strength. The essential position is *not* how well we can respond, *but how well we can lead.*

Driving forces tend to be "discovered" rather than invented. Through exercises and models, firms can learn what's been driving them to date. Most likely, a hidden structure that either facilitates or presents obstacles to the full expression of the driver can be ferreted out. And if we can discover these structures, we can discover the driving forces that have been surreptitiously operating. Then we can work with them. Rather than seeking simple discovery and refinement, some firms go well beyond that point, to revolutionize things with a brand-new driving force. Over the course of several years, a firm in the Northwest executed a well-designed strategic planning and positioning process, culminating in successfully moving from a cost/quality-driven firm to a cutting-edge design leader in their region.

When you decide to make a stand on your driving force, you'll foster certain values and weed out others, using care and patience. You'll fine-tune your entire business model, including staffing, marketing, project systems, and perhaps your ownership structure. Once this model is in focus and consensus is built, you almost can't help but bring the more powerful vision into reality. It becomes that clear.

TABLE 3-2: Essential Linkages from Driving Force to Typical Hidden Agenda, by Archetype

Archetypes	Driving Force	Hidden Client Agenda
Einstein	Innovation	Needs to fulfill need for prestige, improved image
Niche Expert	Cutting-edge Method	Needs to overcome risky, adverse conditions
Market Partner	Client Partnership	Needs to augment client's own skills, as full-services "partner"
Community Leader	Community Contribution	Needs facilitation through community gatekeepers
Orchestrator	Project Management Challenge	Needs to control project complexity
Builder	Cost/Quality Challenge	Needs to deliver the product, optimizing the budget

The Path to Purpose: Driving Forces and the Hidden Client Agenda

The beauty of an identity is that it acts like a magnet to attract a group of clients seeking your kind of expertise. In other words, certain client groupings have typical agendas for which they need certain kinds of firms. See Table 3-2. Rarely do clients go outside their unspoken agendas, and if they do, they tend *not* to recognize value. It's tricky to determine what the client views as most valuable; in fact, some don't consciously know it themselves. Sure, they want and need everything it takes to do their project. But certain aspects will be more critical than others. Needless to say, it's wise to spend time on this question and get real answers. Go beyond the first blush of what the client tells you. Push beyond the shorthand clichés: *be faster*, *be cheaper*, and *give us good service*. Question if these are the most highly charged client needs, or if they're just the outside layer of the onion. Whatever your chosen client values most highly—and you find a worthwhile challenge—make your firm the ultimate expert in that.

Driving Forces and the Sacred Technology

Very specific methodologies for what needs to be done characterize each of the types in *The SPARKS Framework Assessment*. These are the true centers of excellence for which the firm is valued in the marketplace. They are links

TABLE 3-3: Adding the "Sacred Technology" to the Mix

Archetypes	Driving Force	Hidden Client Agenda	Sacred Technology
Einstein	Innovation	Needs to fulfill need for prestige, improved image	Generating brand-new ideas and technologies
Niche Expert	Cutting-edge Method	Needs to overcome risky, adverse conditions	Transferring new knowledge to the target niche
Market Partner	Client Partnership	Needs to augment client's own skills, as full-services "partner"	Expanding ways to help the sector-specific client
Community Leader	Community Connectivity	Needs facilitation through community gatekeepers	Nurturing the network of relationships with local leaders
Orchestrator	Project Management Challenge	Needs to control project complexity	Pushing sophisticated logistics control on large projects
Builder	Cost/Quality Challenge	Needs to deliver the product, optimizing the budget	Advancing brilliant new production technologies

on the overall project value chain, and it's a rare client that considers them all equally valuable.

Ask yourself this question: Are you so busy getting the work in and out that you neglect to nurture the more difficult and risky technology that makes you special? When the firm's driving force is clear, and its leaders understand what's most valuable to its clients, then its Sacred Technology also becomes clear. Table 3-3 lists the Sacred Technology for each type of firm.

Business Design—The Intersection of Strategy and Structure

Curiously, many design firms are themselves not designed. They simply do their clients' bidding and react to whatever is needed at the time. Some firms inadvertently build a business design that is dysfunctional, with lots of structural obstacles in the way of success. Perhaps you know a firm that wanted to build deep community relationships, but the leaders were introverted technical folks. Some firms want to build their project management expertise, but have a chronic fear of becoming "paper pushers." Some want to master a specialty service, but feel they must be *flexible*.

Beyond choosing the firm's identity, the next essential element is a conscious design of the business such that it can play at its peak. When a firm is "playing the game well," it's using a scaffold of practices that are both cohesive and aligned. Things aren't in conflict; they're in *flow*. These elements are the essentials of a positioning plan, and are required to ensure that the firm meets its longer term goals.

Although we can't see what's supporting this desired state, the firm is working with a very specific web of internal strategies and structures that constitute an understood operating model or business design. In a healthy situation, they encourage the desired behaviors and inhibit the undesired behaviors, on a fairly effortless basis. Business designs that inform positioning strategies are powerful shapers of behavior.

Strategic planning, if done correctly, is the process that helps the firm think through its business design and make deliberate decisions about the needs of the overall firm system. Some people think the end result of strategic planning is a sequential list of tasks to be implemented, but a list is ineffectual compared with a business design that uses positioning as the platform for development.

As a macro view of the six archetypes, the chart in Figure 3.1 depicts the continuum of time that might equal a range of 20–25 years. In other words, it gives a generational view of how an emerging design trend or facility type might move through the hands of each operating model. The curved line represents the market growth for the trend, starting small with the Einsteins, peaking with the Market Partners, and moving into a lengthy decline as the design trend becomes commoditized.

The Hierarchy of Business Design

In the framework, each of the six archetypes relies on a distinct business design. And each business design is organized into three distinct strands that form the structural elements of the design. The three strands are in fact primary strategic systems that operate in every firm.

1. **Getting Work:** Markets, Positioning, and Marketing
2. **Doing Work:** Projects, Technology, and People
3. **Organizing Resources:** Money, Organization Design, and Leadership

Broadly speaking, we can use a continuum to array these strategies and activities, ranging from the Einsteins and Niche Experts at one end, to the Orchestrators and Builders at the other. A macro view only, the chart in Table 3-4 illustrates the range of these basic practices. For example, when the archetypes at the left seek higher visibility, they increase their writing,

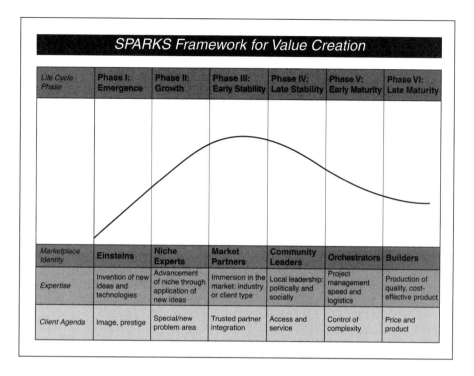

Life Cycle Phase	Phase I: Emergence	Phase II: Growth	Phase III: Early Stability	Phase IV: Late Stability	Phase V: Early Maturity	Phase VI: Late Maturity
Marketplace Identity	Einsteins	Niche Experts	Market Partners	Community Leaders	Orchestrators	Builders
Expertise	Invention of new ideas and technologies	Advancement of niche through application of new ideas	Immersion in the market: industry or client type	Local leadership: politically and socially	Project management speed and logistics	Production of quality, cost-effective product
Client Agenda	Image, prestige	Special/new problem area	Trusted partner integration	Access and service	Control of complexity	Price and product

Figure 3.1   The SPARKS Framework graph denotes the six major archetypal choices for firm identity. The horizontal line represents how new ideas and project types expand early in their developmental cycles, then tail off as market saturation and commoditization occurs. (*Source: Creating Wealth: Principles and Practices for Design Firms* by Ellen Flynn-Heapes, 2000)

teaching, and speaking. When the archetypes at the right seek higher visibility, they benefit more from exhibits, direct mail, and advertising. When the firms at the left seek to improve their work, they try more experimentation and collaboration, while their colleagues at the right focus on greater utilization and productivity. When the firms at the left seek to track their

TABLE 3-4: The Best Practices Continuum

	Einsteins	Niche Experts	Market Partners	Community Leaders	Orchestrators	Builders
Getting Work	Writing, Teaching, & Speaking ◁----------▷ Exhibits, Direct Mail, Ads					
Doing Work	Experimentation & Collaboration ◁----------▷ Utilization and Productivity					
Organizing Resources	Design Performance Statistics ◁----------▷ Budget and Schedule Statistics					

TABLE 3-5: Firm Subsystems

Getting Work: Markets, Positioning, and Marketing	*What Is the Firm Known for?* Sales Message Promotional Strategy Geographic Reach Best Fees
Doing Work: Projects, Technology, and People	*What Are the Firm's Targets?* Deep Expertise Staff Mix Project Management Learning
Organizing Resources: Money, Organization Design, and Leadership	*How Does the Firm Organize for Business?* Ownership Investments Offices Information Systems

performance, they look for design-related statistics, while their colleagues at the right aim for budget and schedule statistics.

In application, we set strategy not only in the broad systems but also in the subsystems. The basic subsystems of most firms are listed in Table 3-5.

The following business designs (Figures 3.2–3.7 and Tables 3-6–3-11) are based on extensive research and practical experience with successful design firms throughout the country. Experience shows that these organizations are most successful when their strategies are aligned with one model, rather than a blend of various models.

That being said, most firms find themselves practicing under several models. We see hybrids, for example, of Market Partners using a niche strategy, Orchestrators using a Community Leader strategy, and so forth. However, the best choice is to be firmly anchored in one character type, and then cross-fertilize in a deliberately designed way.

The Challenge of Multiple Markets

It's no surprise that the majority of firms take on projects spanning more than one specific market. Although there are many firms that are dedicated to markets such as K–12, hospitality, or municipal, this level of specialization is still fairly rare. The reasons for this diversification are straightforward: Principals/partners have interests and experience in certain markets, and

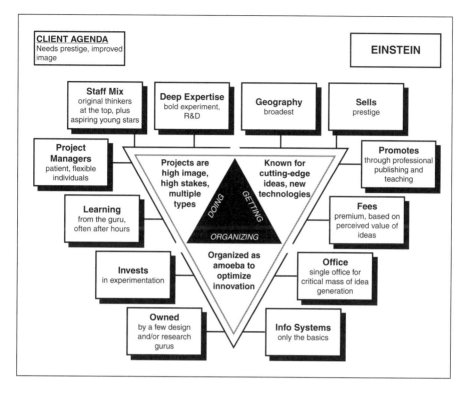

Figure 3.2   The Einstein archetype fits best when a firm is seeking to lead in design innovation and big ideas.

TABLE 3-6: Einstein

Client Agenda	Needs prestige, improved image
Client Value	Cutting-edge ideas or technologies
Getting Work ***Known for cutting-edge ideas***	***Geography***: Broadest ***Sells***: Prestige ***Promotes***: Teaching/publishing ***Fees***: Premium, perceived value of ideas
Doing Work ***High-image, high-stakes, multiple types***	***Deep expertise***: Bold experiment, R&D ***Staff***: Original thinkers, aspiring stars ***PM***: Patient, flexible ***Learning***: From guru, often after hours
Organizing Resources ***Organized as an amoeba to optimize innovation***	***Invests***: Experimentation ***Owned***: One primary, or a few gurus ***Info Systems***: Basics ***Office***: Single, critical mass of ideas

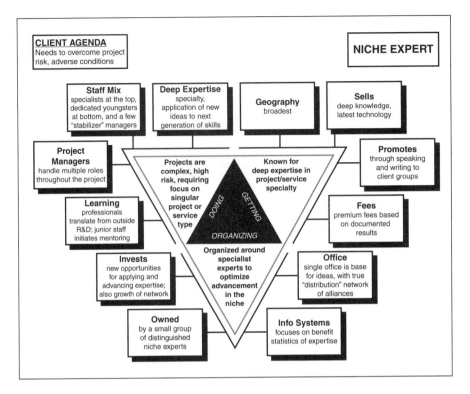

Figure 3.3 A Niche Expert typically chooses a limited market scope and only offers a few project types.

TABLE 3-7: Niche Expert

Client Agenda	Needs to overcome project risk, adverse conditions
Client Value	Unsurpassed leadership in a specific area
Getting Work **Known for deep expertise in project or service specialty**	**Geography**: Broadest **Sells**: Rare knowledge **Promotes**: Speaking/writing to client groups **Fees**: Premium, documented results
Doing Work **Complex or high-risk, singular type**	**Deep expertise**: Latest approaches **Staff**: Specialists at top, dedicated youngsters and stabilizers in middle **PM**: Dedicated specialists who can also handle the realities of the management process **Learning**: Juniors initiate mentoring
Organizing Resources **Organized around specialists to optimize advancement of the niche**	**Invests**: New applications, depth of network **Owned**: Distinguished experts **Info Systems**: Benefit statistics **Office**: Single for critical mass, alliances

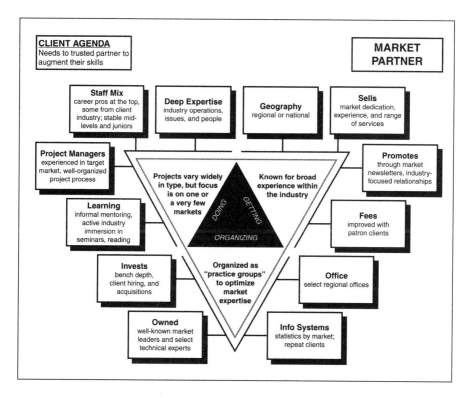

Figure 3.4 The Market Partner is an operating model in which the firm wants to develop a balance of market expertise, long-term client relationships, and a wide scope of services.

TABLE 3-8: Market Partner

Client Agenda	Needs a trusted partner, augment skills
Client Value	Service depth within a market area
Getting Work ***Known for broad experience within an industry***	***Geography***: Regional or national ***Sells***: Market dedication, experience, access ***Promotes***: Industry connections, trend letters ***Fees***: Improved with patron clients
Doing Work ***Range of types within one or few markets***	***Deep expertise***: Industry operations, people ***Staff***: Stable array of professionals, some from within client industry ***PM***: Well organized, experienced in market ***Learning***: Conventions, informal mentors
Organizing Resources ***Organized as practice groups to optimize market expertise***	***Invests***: Bench depth, like-firm acquisitions ***Owned***: Known market players, select techs ***Info Systems***: Stats by market, repeat clients ***Office***: Select regional offices

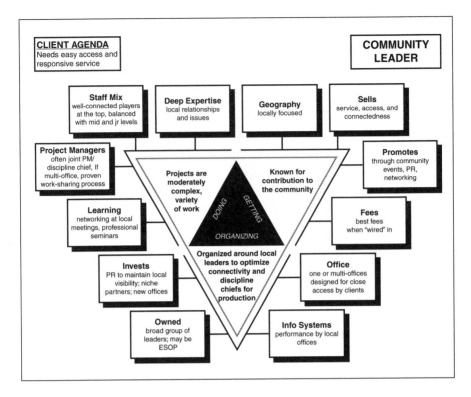

Figure 3.5 The Community Leader model relies on strong political and social connections to gain access to clients and address a broad range of local project needs.

TABLE 3-9: Community Leader

Client Agenda	Needs access and service
Client Value	Mutual commitment to community
Getting Work **Known for contribution to the community**	**Geography**: Community-based **Sells**: Access, service, connectedness **Promotes**: Community events, PR, network **Fees**: Improved when "wired in"
Doing Work **Range of types, moderate complexity**	**Deep expertise**: Local relationships, issues **Staff:** Multidiscipline groups **PM**: Combined PM/discipline chiefs; if large firm, has strong work-sharing process **Learning**: Networking locally, professionally
Organizing Resources **Organized around local leaders to optimize connectivity**	**Invests**: Local visibility, niche partners, new offices **Owned**: Broad group, may be ESOP **Info Systems**: Performance by local office **Office**: One or multi, for local access

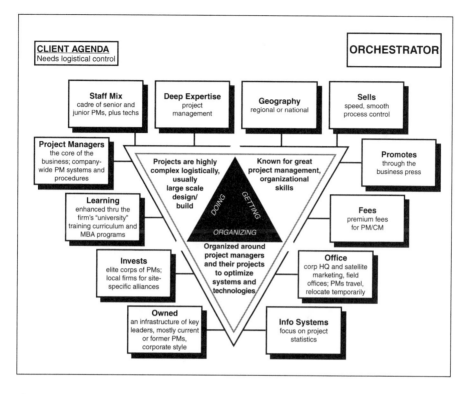

Figure 3.6 The Orchestrator archetype develops strong technical and project management skills and services to meet the demands of complex projects.

TABLE 3-10: Orchestrator

Client Agenda	Needs logistical control
Client Value	Skilled PM for larger, complex projects
Getting Work ***Known for great project management,*** ***organizational skills***	***Geography***: Regional or national ***Sells***: Speed, process control ***Promotes***: Through business press ***Fees***: Premium fees for PM/CM
Doing Work ***Highly complex logistically, larger scale,*** ***often design/build***	***Deep expertise***: PM ***Staff:*** Senior and jr. PMs, MBAs ***PM***: Top PM systems, tools, resources ***Learning***: Formal training curriculum
Organizing Resources ***Organized around PMs to optimize systems*** ***and technologies***	***Invests***: Elite corps of PMs, local firm alliances ***Owned***: Current or former PMs, corporate ***Info Systems***: Project-level statistics ***Office***: Corp. HQ plus satellites; PMs travel

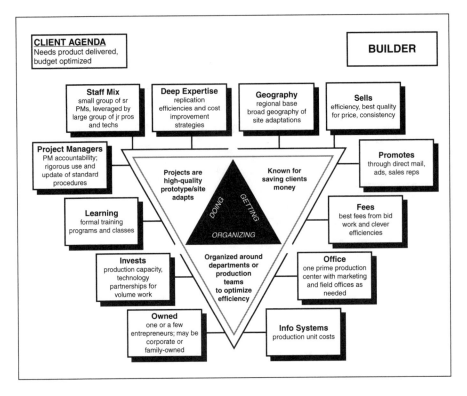

Figure 3.7 The Builder relies on strong planning and project control capabilities in order to deliver multiple units of work on time and within budget.

TABLE 3-11: Builder

Client Agenda	Needs product delivered, budget optimized
Client Value	Cost, quality, and consistency
Getting Work ***Known for quality work at a low cost***	***Geography***: Regional base, broad site alliances ***Sells***: Best quality for price, consistency ***Promotes***: Direct mail, ads, sales reps ***Fees***: Bid work, clever efficiencies
Doing Work ***Mostly prototype/site adaptations***	***Deep expertise***: Replication efficiencies ***Staff:*** Jr. professionals and techs ***PM***: Accountability, standard procedures ***Learning***: Formal training classes
Organizing Resources ***Organized around production teams to optimize efficiency***	***Invests***: Production capacity, technology ***Owned***: One or a few entrepreneurs, may be family-owned ***Info Systems***: Production unit costs ***Office***: Production center, field offices

wish to continue to build their reputation in those arenas. Another reason is that the firm's early days were defined by the clients who chose them, not the other way around. The need to get the firm established and profitable greatly outweighs any considerations of developing firm-wide market expertise. Finally, there's the fear factor. Firm owners are unwilling to put all their eggs in one basket, given the potential for downward market shifts, economic instability, and other events that cannot be easily predicted. While competitive pressures also play a role in this diversity, all these conditions tend to mask the nature of the opportunities offered by a sharper market focus. Over time, these normal and natural inclinations begin to exact a price from the firm, especially as more specialized competitors pitch their services to clients wanting more than a good list of design-related capabilities. So the question remains: How can a firm be considered more of a specialist and not take on all the risks associated with the potential reversal of the market they choose? What are the tricks to managing in multiple markets without appearing diluted in the eyes of clients who want specialized knowledge and expertise?

There are two good answers to these questions. First, firms should consider centering their practice around a sector, such as hospitality. Within hospitality, there are numerous segments including hotels, restaurants, retail, resorts, and senior living facilities. Services such as landscape architecture, interior design, and lighting design—whether provided in-house or through partners—can be strategically developed to position the firm as a leader in that sector. To the extent that sectors do experience downturns and shifts in availability of project work, most of these clients continue to seek out firms that will remain committed to their needs over time. Certainly, a strong argument can be made that "living with" a client set during tough times can actually unearth new types of projects and additional services, and the firm needs to stay positioned for these over the long haul. As more firms develop their roles as dedicated specialists in a field, it's becoming harder to abandon a market where you have a modest resume, and then return to it once things improve in a few years.

The second answer to the dilemma is to design the firm in a way that fully comprehends the requirements of being in multiple and disconnected markets, such as combining hospitality with science and technology work. This approach demands that the firm look at each sector as its own separate business, and build the identity, operating model, strategy, and positioning system in a unique fashion for each line of business. As a result, the firm may choose the archetype of Niche Expert for one sector, while taking on the role of Market Partner for another sector. The mindsets, internal systems, marketing approaches, and client service programs for each of these operating models will vary greatly, and need to be designed and managed accordingly. Most firms do not function with this clarity, failing to make critical distinctions about the identity and operating model elements needed to support the projects they pursue. Instead, the firm can turn into a convoluted mix of various beliefs, approaches, and servicing models that destroys the potential strength offered by clear identity choices.

Even the most successful design firms come to a major intersection where they must answer deeper questions about their identity and purpose. Very often, there's one individual who carves out the path for others to follow, and an entirely new vision begins to unfold. This is the situation that developed at a Central New York firm over the past few years.

CASE STUDY: BLUE DESIGN, A NEW IDENTITY AND PURPOSE PATH FOR ASHLEY MCGRAW ARCHITECTS

Expanding a firm's identity may seem easy on paper, but when it comes to putting all the pieces of the puzzle together, it means a new level of commitment that transcends the next good idea. Ashley McGraw Architects, a Syracuse, New York, firm with over 30 years of history behind them, has learned this lesson well. As a 75-person firm, they have doubled in size over the past six years, a necessity for their continued success in the K–12 and college and university marketplace. From a need to become more strategically focused, they have evolved to become a firm with a mission—a higher purpose—that, according to CEO Ed McGraw, is just what the doctor ordered. "We had been doing great work, and frankly, we were satisfied, but that was all rear view mirror thinking. We knew we needed a catalyst to move us ahead again, and it took Pete to make it happen."

Meet Pete, head of the Advanced Building Studio (ABS) at Ashley McGraw. Peter Larson, AIA, LEED AP, is principal and founder of the studio, and a driving force shaping the future of the firm. According to Larson, he was ready to make some changes. "I had grown a bit restless with just the next project we had to work on. I knew I had the opportunity to do more with my life, and make a significant contribution to the firm. After some soul-searching, it was clear to me that the status quo of being just a little better than the next firm down the street wasn't enough. We needed—I needed—to create a new paradigm for all of us to move forward in a big way."

That new paradigm is Blue Design, Pete's brainchild, and the path the entire firm has begun following. As Pete says, "Blue Design isn't just the next round of green or sustainable architecture, it's an entirely new way of thinking about our relationship with nature, resources and the possibilities of design." As he wrote in the preface of his recently published booklet, *Blue Design: An Elegant Path to the Future*, "Blue Design was created using an atypical approach. Many solutions are developed from the bottom up, relying on the invention of a new building component, manufacturing process, or efficiency improvement to reduce the resource consumption of a larger assembly. This approach improves resource performance by a varying degree that is ultimately limited by the paradigm it was created within; in the present case the industrial paradigm. Blue Design was created using an opposite, top-down approach; moving outside of architecture and the industrial paradigm, away from specific project-based solutions and towards encompassing philosophical and systemic concepts."

These core beliefs, plus a good dose of personal initiative and the support of the firm, have led to the firm's adoption of an entirely new purpose for the work they perform. It does include specific aspects of net zero energy goals and renewable energy strategies, but it's really a bigger picture than that. The true goal of Blue Design is to effect changes to the very system that is assumed to be the only one we have. Instead of making small adjustments, the approach offers a top-down set of tools and analytical processes that aren't a checklist or a one-size-fits-all solution.

In addition to the role that the Advanced Building Studio has developed, bigger elements are also in the picture, including the establishment of an institute to lead in discovery and maturation of the thinking behind Blue Design. The overall vision integrates ABS, the institute, and the firm, as drawn up in the role definitions given in Figure 3.8.

With such major implications for the firm at stake, the leaders decided to hold a two-day retreat in the fall of 2009 to fully explain the philosophy, begin the alignment process, and get feedback from

The Three Components and Their Roles

The Blue Design Institute (BDI)
Create - Blue Design
Gather - diverse disciplines
Communicate - Blue Design to wide audiences
Research - non-project environment solutions
Maintain - the Solution Framework
Distribute - Blue Design collaborators and solutions for in-project application

The Advanced Building Studio (ABS)
Translate - BDI-developed solutions into project environments
Diffuse - new BD solutions to AM project staff
Implement - BD solutions in project environments
Quantity - energy and resource performance in project environments
Consult - with outside professional clients for resource modeling

Ashley McGraw Architects (AM)
Blend-Blue Design with the other aspects of being a great firm:
- ○ Client service
- ○ Quality product
- ○ Excellent project management
- ○ High design
- ○ Project profitability
- ○ Market positioning

Embody - the first Blue Design film
Lead - Clients and collaborators in to a new way of thinking

Figure 3.8 Careful integration of the traditional work of the firm with new initiatives is required to create a strong and durable bond. In this example, the institute would focus on outreach and innovation, while the studio works on application development and a solutions framework for the firm's specific clients. (*Source:* Peter Larson, Ashley McGraw Architects)

staff members. The event was a resounding success, ramping up a high level of excitement, curiosity, and ideas for how to proceed. One lengthy breakout session on day one included the establishment of 10 key topic tables, with staff members rotating through in groups to ask questions and offer their thoughts. The results of this were recorded by topic hosts, who presented a summary to all attendees, essentially outlining many elements of what the firm's strategy will be for the next 10 years. One sample from those summaries is the points made regarding creativity and innovation:

- Blue Design requires a forum for free-flowing thoughts.
- Blue Design charettes with full participation.

- We need flex space, project centers, team involvement.
- Risk and failure are inherent in Blue Design.
- Understanding of risk must be top-down.
- We need partner involvement, good communication.
- Blue Design "takes the lid off the process." How will it change how we perform our work?
- The only constant is change. We must be willing to take the risk: WE HAVE TO DO THIS.
- The process cannot be linear. Blue Design will require full team/ABS/consultant/X Factor elements from the beginning.
- We must help to make people/clients more comfortable with the discomfort of exploring new territory.
- Creativity and innovation will require brainstorming and free thinking. Take a more organic approach, increase scale of sharing.
- Market our Blue Design creativity and innovation.
- Establish www.bluedesign.org.
- Look at other cutting-edge design firms; encourage "open sourcing" for the good of all.

In concert with the high-level ideas behind the new philosophy, the entire firm is taking a close look at their major market, K–12 schools. As Larson says, "We are at the beginning of a decline in the availability of fossil fuels. Much of our way of life was founded on the use of cheap energy. *Improved methods of thinking in the old ways* about energy cannot solve this problem. We must approach this issue with new thinking, using all the technology at our disposal, and treat this fundamental shift as an opportunity to find different, new, better, less energy intensive ways to maintain our standard of living." Key aspects of this exploration include asking, "What will the K–12 school be like in the coming age of declining fossil fuel (FF) availability and rapidly rising fossil fuel costs?" The ABS, to this point, has been focusing on developing net zero fossil fuel energy solutions that apply only to the operational energy of the building. This is only one aspect of the total impact. The movement away from a society fueled by cheap energy creates dramatic changes in all aspects of life, including how we teach our children and how our schools function at a fundamental level. The following are some of the other possible impacts to the school in the coming era of declining fossil fuel availability:

- Changes in the school day/week/year: longer/fewer school days, longer winter and summer breaks at peak heating/cooling energy demand. Many repercussions for instructional structure will come from this trend.
- The return of the neighborhood school could reduce transportation distances.
- Remote teaching could reduce the need for transportation.
- Where will learning occur? Will it be remote, home-based learning, or "nodal" learning at a neighborhood level with remote teachers?
- Increased viability of renewable energy: different scenarios for powering electric devices vs. heating/cooling. Substantial investments are required to install renewable energy.
- Rising transportation costs affect offsite activities such as sports, field trips, etc.
- A move away from FF-intensive building materials and construction practices could change the way schools are built.
- Increased emphasis on building and material reuse could reduce FF-intensive material costs (balanced by efficiency upgrades).
- School menus may change to reflect a movement away from energy-intensive foods. Increasing incorporation of local, seasonal menus is already starting to occur at some schools. The average vegetable consumes 10 calories of FF agricultural energy to produce 1 calorie of nutritional energy, because of chemical use, agricultural machinery, storage, and transportation energy.
- Curricular changes: The end of cheap FF energy will affect all aspects of our society. The curriculum will need to change to reflect this.
- Consolidation of schools with other public uses could take place.

While the firm's new approach to thinking about the future resonates with tremendous hope and possibility, Larson is also a realist. He understands that it's a long road, and there will be numerous zigs and zags along the way. But as he says, "I knew this was too important not to pursue, both for myself and Ashley McGraw. What's nice is that my own search for mid-career inspiration and a greater purpose has taken hold right here where I always wanted to be. Our firm is a special place, and I know we'll take on this challenge with the same energy and commitment we have for everything else we do."

Some firm identities are developed as a function of being a team player and partner. Being valued as a technical specialist can also include respecting the boundaries of the client-partner relationship. The following firm has made that a priority for their growing practice.

CASE STUDY: HOW POSITIONING AS A PARTNER DRIVES GEODESIGN'S MARKETING PROGRAM

GeoDesign, Inc., headquartered in Middlebury, Connecticut, with offices in New York City and Vermont, had been enjoying steady growth over its first 10 years in business since its founding in 1995. It built a strong reputation based on the founders' previous experience working for large geotechnical and environmental engineering firms.

Those founders, Ted von Rosenvinge, PE, and Ulrich LaFosse, PE, were well known in the industry as professionals who used innovation combined with practicality to make it possible for even the most challenging geotechnical and environmental projects to be built safely, while maintaining economic focus. In fact, they coined the term "Constructible Innovation" for their firm's tag line. While Ulrich's strengths are in the technology and internal financial management areas, Ted used his natural marketing acumen to lead the firm's business development efforts. "Other firms seemed to grow for the sake of growing; we wanted to maintain focus," explains Ted. "We felt we would expand naturally and in a controlled way by simply providing outstanding service direct from the firm's principals, applying innovative approaches to project challenges, and building and developing the right team."

By 2006, the firm had grown to 20 staff members in its 10 years and enjoyed a strong backlog of work. "We realized we weren't in

Kansas any more, so to speak," said Ted. "We had to formalize our systems and step up efforts if we were to sustain the firm's growth. We knew we had to change to evolve." Today the firm has a staff of 40.

In late 2006, they conducted their first formal strategic marketing plan, utilizing an external consulting firm. The initial analysis revealed that the firm possessed strong leadership committed to the success of the firm and the best interests of the entire GeoDesign team. They had a low overhead rate as compared to similar firms in the industry, which helped boost their profit level to within the industry's upper quartile. To take them to the next level, however, the firm needed clearer roles, additional structure, and more staff. They also needed to put additional efforts into marketing.

The firm identified key client types and assigned each to a principal-level market leader, who would be responsible for overseeing the marketing efforts for the target group. In addition, Ted identified a younger shareholder who had a flare for and interest in marketing—a natural to support the firm's marketing efforts. The key was to position the firm as a niche provider based on its successful "Constructible Innovation" brand.

With this marketing focus, the firm instituted a more comprehensive and visual representation of the brand. Renewed emphasis on the brand was applied to an updated corporate brochure, a more regularly produced newsletter, and the firm's website. The yearly calendar was upgraded for 2010 to proudly display the brand, and featured interesting, noteworthy client projects. It garnered tremendous positive feedback from clients and project team members who wanted their projects to be featured in a future calendar.

Press releases and articles were produced on a more regular schedule, award submittals increased, and the firm's principals were quoted more often in national-level publications, and even on a syndicated radio talk show on WCBS 880 AM, New York City. The firm had chosen New York City as a focal point for diversifying their geographic footprint beyond central Connecticut. Ted explains:

> During this uptick in marketing efforts, we stuck to our knitting. We remain true to our niche and avoid competition with our project team members. We've turned down opportunities to expand into other areas, such as bridge and roadway design. Instead, we defer

such opportunities to our design clients and often later serve the contractors who build such facilities. Niche positioning and discipline to stay within our niche have been hallmarks of our controlled growth.

When the economy slowed, GeoDesign had already established a diverse mix of clients, and that diversity was critical to sustaining the firm's level of business. Years before the recent economic slowdown, firm leaders had skillfully identified construction engineering services to contractors as a niche market that was underserved. This market is also more infrastructure-oriented and less susceptible to swings in the real estate market. In addition, GeoDesign's construction engineering services have become a fast-growing and profitable market. These services go beyond traditional geotechnical engineering into geostructural, environmental, and construction consulting.

Even with the stagnant economic environment in 2009, the firm has put together some impressive results. According to Ted, having all the firm's key forces pushing in one direction has been the key. He explains: "Our billings increased by 11 percent in 2009 after a 16 percent increase the year previous. We've maintained our staff size while adding four new major clients. We've increased LEED accreditation by three staff, and invested in a formal leadership development program for our senior managers. And some exciting new areas have been developed, including new technology applications for onsite remediation of contamination as well as flood protection levee assessments that have become a real need since Katrina hit."

With all these accomplishments adding up in a relatively short timeframe, both founders are convinced that their decision to position the firm as a supportive partner will continue to pay dividends.

NOW FOR SALE: OUR CULTURE, OUR PROCESSES

Beyond the world of design, fast-growing companies are modeling a new approach to creating their identity. One such example is Zappos, the online shoe retailer that prides itself on its customer service, and is eager to give away its secrets to anyone who cares to listen. As an "open innovator," Zappos is giving personality and style to the world of online service.

Stepping outside the design industry, there are many examples of companies that create unique and compelling identities that propel their business model to great heights. In a world that has exploded with information over the past two decades, it should come as no surprise that companies are no longer afraid that competitors will find out their secrets of success. Long gone are the days when such secrets would be hidden like rare jewels—in fact, the price today can be as little as $39.95 a month, the amount Zappos charges for website membership to learn about their way of doing business.

Zappos.com is a leader in online shoe selling, and it also leads in playfulness and fun, a model that has drawn significant attention from clients and competitors alike. *Zappos Insights*, a monthly online newsletter the firm is launching, is designed to offer management videos and tips from staff. The company also provides two-day seminars on how to reproduce the essence of its corporate culture. As the tours proceed through the call center in Las Vegas, staffers blow horns and ring cowbells to greet the visitors as they attempt to absorb the environment and creativity that has made Zappos famous. For seminar attendees, it's an open book, as CEO Tony Hsieh and his team cover aspects of how they run the company, including recruiting, compensation, client care, and creating the right working environment. This may seem a bit too altruistic, but it's all about building the Zappos brand. The company will go to great lengths to fix a client complaint, realizing that in a world like theirs, which "lives" online, the chance to win over a client for good may last only the space of one phone call.

And the good news is, it's working—so well, in fact, that Amazon, the largest online retailer, paid $847 million for the firm in 2009. Because while Zappos is busy giving away how they do what they do, Amazon is also offering its business model and processes to other firms for a fee, all to push the further integration of Amazon into the broader online experience.

Can a design firm emulate any of these approaches and ideas? The answer is likely a *yes*. Any firm that feels they have developed successful approaches to problem solving, project management, or client satisfaction can make a splash by branding what they do. Consider going upstream the next time your firm works for a client. Let them see your design talent when it comes to your proposal and presentation—wow them with the graphics and attention-grabbing layout of the material. Design a mock-up showing how their own marketing materials could look for their new project, and let them know you're prepared to take on this task as part of your package of services. Land the first client or two like this, and then issue a press release announcing your new service. Post what you do and how you do it, on your website, and soon, just like Zappos, you'll be known for offering more than the most basic design services. The cowbells are optional, of course.

CONDUCTING A STAFF RETREAT TO ADDRESS POSITIONING AND FIRM IDENTITY

For any firm wishing to position itself for the future, the first real goal is to get the staff on board. Beyond the needs to make the "intellectual decisions" relative to markets, services, and marketing strategies, the ultimate prize cannot be captured without the passion and production of the staff. Although affordability is always an issue, the best approach is to get the team off-site for a day or two and immerse them in thinking about the "Who are we?" and "Where are we going?" questions.

An agenda for a staff retreat has many possible topics and options. There may be a guest speaker, perhaps a tour of a local facility, and enough time set aside to allow the staff to explore issues and ideas through exercises and small workshops. There is likely to be an opening session that looks back on the history of the firm, acknowledges the accomplishments, and poses the key questions that remain for the future.

Once that's done, senior staff members may present some details relative to the big ideas that can propel the firm forward. These presentations might relate to markets, services, client relations, or many of the standard topics. However, the best approaches are typically more exploratory in nature. What are the emerging angles of technology, society, and the economy that are affecting us now and will in the future? What philosophies grab our attention when it comes to our firm's ultimate purpose and mission? How can we articulate the parts of these trends that are most meaningful to the firm and make them our own?

These are big questions for any firm to ponder at any point in time. Yet, the shifts that have occurred in recent years demand that we pull back a bit and take in the larger horizon. Is it enough to become LEED certified or meet the current educational requirements for structural engineers? Are we able to remain competitive if our efforts are mostly geared to chasing work—work that is now being chased by many more firms than just a few years ago?

Regardless of where your firm has been, your staff wants to be led by confident leadership expressing big ideas. And while the ideas need to be substantial, the implementation should be measured and deliberate. That's the inherent challenge of taking on a staff retreat that deals with the future, and while it's not simple, it does need to be done.

One aspect of such a retreat is the presentation addressing the marketing and PR aspects of the firm. This should include at least five sections, as follows:

- Primary goals of the program
- Where we have been
- Where we are now
- What you will see in the future
- The ultimate benefits

Each of these sections contains a wide array of possible discussion points. Let's take each one individually, to develop a sample approach.

Primary Goals

In most cases, the firm will be challenged to create a stronger marketing presence, often newly defined by aspects of the chosen "big idea" (sustainability, for example). The firm needs to be able to express its new role in relation to its key markets, and display how those markets are shifting their priorities and needs. A key goal will be to increase the firm's recognition, both for its forward-looking ideas and for past accomplishments. Another goal will be to successfully navigate the integration of past and future positions in the market. Lastly, a somewhat operational goal may be established, such as "becoming more PR and news driven."

Regardless of which big idea drives the firm for the next 10 years, these primary goals should remain stable and consistent. Staff groups need that stability to begin to find their new place in that future firm, and shifting sands only serve to undermine that process.

Where We Have Been

Discussion points in this section include a brief history of the marketing organization and people, showing how they have evolved over the years. Recognize key contributors, and delineate the progression of roles and responsibilities. Along with these, the primary functional activities are described, ranging from proposal development to arranging speaking and writing opportunities. Successes should also be mentioned, and these can include a few key projects, notable marketing programs, and events that have elevated the firm's recognition in the industry. Lastly, there are always holes in past performance that need to be filled. Describing these will keep the presentation grounded in the reality of the firm's current position, and emphasize that it needs to sculpt a new, more powerful impression in the marketplace.

Where We Are Now

This idea should often be expressed as a function of entering a transition. When the world changes, we need to change, and this means describing the thought and decision processes that have brought us to this point. An organization in transition needs new skills and resources as well as the new ideas. Utilizing external expertise can help jump-start the process, and announcing this at this moment will help cement the firm's commitment to its future intentions. On a more practical level, issues and the outlines of solutions can be presented. These might include database development, branding, a new website, and the stronger use of PR to transmit the new message to key markets and clients.

What You Will See

The main point of this section is to display the energy and passion that are behind the firm's new direction. New behaviors are described, and new roles are emphasized by firm leaders. Possibilities and the chance for accomplishing significant achievements should be reinforced. All in all, there needs to be a passion for the future, and this is where it becomes real and felt by those in the audience.

The Ultimate Benefits

As with any good presentation, a recap is needed. The staff needs to hear why stronger positioning is necessary for the firm. They need to hear how it will benefit them, and enrich their careers and opportunities. They need to "get" the ideas behind sharpening the firm's competitive advantage. They need to see how increased capabilities in the marketing and PR arena will create a more vibrant and resilient organization. In the end, it is always about the clients, and the markets they inhabit. The firm's efforts will translate into direct benefits for clients as well as staff, and this essential interdependency demands that we take the time—and the risk—to become the firm that meets the challenge of its potential.

SUMMARY

Firm identity and purpose are complicated issues, made easier when firms commit to specific areas of specialization and growth. With so many choices available when it comes to positioning strategies, firm leaders need to be thinking deeply about their greatest aspirations and capabilities—not chasing a wide range of projects that may further commoditize their position in the profession. While many of these decisions are difficult and will take time to bear fruit, they will significantly enhance the firm's chances for moving beyond survival into a state of thriving, as the years fly by.

CHAPTER 4

MARKETS AND SERVICES

When it comes to the topics of markets and services, the elephant in the room for the design industry is sustainability. And rightfully so, as that subject remains a critical consideration from the combined perspectives of energy efficiency, social change, and technological development, as applied to design and construction. The underlying motivation is that unless we rebalance our planet's entire ecosystem, life on earth will enter a much more precarious period. Ten years ago, the larger topic would likely have been globalization, as corporations and firms were in the midst of discovering vast new opportunities in emerging markets. The power of the Internet drove globalization for many industries that previously couldn't piece together a viable methodology for doing business across the U.S., much less on the other side of the world. This isn't to suggest that globalization is waning or won't be on the top of many firms' lists of positioning initiatives. More to the point is the recognition of the fact that global problems and opportunities are a shared pool to consider, as opposed to being primarily influenced by the views and needs of the traditionally dominant Western economies with aggressive corporations and business plans.

For the design industry, these dynamics are important because it's the overall success of these institutions that will provide the funds to develop the sustainability effort, both at home and around the globe. Logic would say that if the best clients are moving more deeply into a global perspective on business, with ambitious plans for building and running more sustainable enterprises, the design industry needs to be right there with them. Of course, the larger design firms will always get most of the press and recognition for their achievements. The question becomes: What do the smaller, lesser-known firms do to position themselves within this broader opportunity? What advances can local or regional firms make to move beyond mimicry of the larger firms, in order to provide their clients with competitive ideas and solutions to the same problems facing the giants of industry? How can "average" clients be brought to higher levels of inspiration and achievement through the development of core sustainability strategies?

For centuries, the world was thought to be flat, but it has now long been known to be round. A number of years ago, Thomas Friedman's book *The World Is Flat*, gave us a fresh perspective on that consideration, within the newly minted planetary system of communication and the merging of worldwide interests and threats. As these advances continue, perhaps the world is actually becoming concave, with all of our cultures, problems, systems, and opportunities bumping into each other around every turn. This convergence of issues and opportunities can certainly be disorienting at times, but it also provides a wealth of opportunity for entities of all types.

Most firm leaders are familiar with, or directly involved in, the explosive growth that has occurred in places most of us have never seen with our own eyes, but some might be surprised by the growth that is still taking place. Consider this excerpt from a March 2010 press release by Godwin Austen Johnson, a UK firm with a large presence in the Middle East and North Africa.

Godwin Austen Johnson expands design team following growth of regional contracts:

Godwin Austen Johnson (GAJ), one of the largest and longest-established UK architectural and design practices in the UAE, has announced a 10 per cent increase in staffing to support new contracts across the Middle East and North Africa.

In line with the firm's business development strategy GAJ has expanded into Tunisia and Libya after securing a number of architectural and design projects. GAJ has also won additional contracts within its largest project Sharm Al Sheikh City Stars—a phased 15-year commercial, residential, retail and leisure development in Egypt which, when complete, will be the size of Wales and will contain the world's largest swimming pool.

GAJ has appointed 10 architects and interior designers, primarily from within the UAE, to support the growth in business. The new recruits will work on a range of large mixed use developments comprising hospitality, commercial and residential elements as well as existing projects that have increased in scope.

GAJ attributes its recent success to a considered approach to business diversification and regional expansion. The firm now has over 180 staff at its offices in Dubai, Abu Dhabi, Sharjah and the UK and offers a wide range of expertise in architecture, interior design, graphic design and structural engineering to meet the demands of the fast-developing economies across the region.

"The MENA region appears to have weathered the economic storm that we have seen globally over the past two years better than most. The countries that make up the region are still developing many aspects of their economies and the projects that we are undertaking there are reflections of this," said Brian Johnson, Principal and Managing Partner of GAJ.

With its multi-disciplinary design offering, GAJ has been able to bring financial and time efficiencies to clients—another boon in the current business climate. In Libya the firm was awarded the contract for interior design as well as for the branding of a 7-star hotel and says its integrated design capabilities are already reaping dividends for the client.

Within the Middle East, GAJ seeks to create a marriage of contemporary design with traditional Arabic and Islamic influences. Its distinctive approach to design continues to attract new business opportunities from across the region as well as recognition from the industry. Most recently GAJ was awarded Middle East Architectural Firm of the Year (modern architecture category) at the Middle East Architect's Awards 2009.

For some readers, this may simply represent another example of regional excess that mirrors aspects of the U.S. excesses that have recently gone quiet. However, a closer examination of the release and of the GAJ website reveals the essentials of what makes a firm successful: a willingness to invest in the long-term prospects of a specific market, and the commitment to offering in-depth services that require layers of talent to conceive and execute. Against a backdrop of a fairly high-risk environment, GAJ and other firms are growing, against the grain of the current belief system of much of the design world. Firms that stick with and hone their essential principles and beliefs, regardless of temporary financing problems, will win the day when the system has righted itself.

MARKET SELECTION, PENETRATION, AND INFLUENCE

Once a design firm has been in existence for about 10 years, it discovers a pressing need to better define its reason for being. After a reasonably lengthy period of practice, some doubts begin to surface about future performance, and confidence in the founders' decisions can come into question. If the economic conditions are right, these uncertainties will be brushed under the carpet. But when business conditions weaken, there will be a rush of questions about the firm's true purpose. Are we in the right markets? Can we influence our clients' thinking enough to win the projects we truly want to work on? If not, how do we make the shift into a stronger position, one that allows us to create great projects from something that was just another generic facility?

Much like maturing individuals, firms move through a number of important stages that determine their ultimate fate. In adolescence, they may try a great number of alternative paths towards success, conquering a few but failing at most. Approaching middle age, they experience an earned appreciation for the meaning of the effort, and perhaps a renewal of dedication towards the essential craft of their chosen profession. As this stage wears on, however, they may find that other firms—the dreaded, lurking competition—have been renewing themselves at a greater pace. They have been narrowing their choice of markets significantly, and hiring the kind of talent that makes heads turn. They are appearing at an increasing number of important conferences as speakers, and penning articles that not only make great sense, but also display a confidence of leadership that project experience alone cannot engender. In short, our firm begins to feel that time is passing us by, and the sense of urgency about future prospects increases. So the question remains: How does a firm seeking recognition and longevity, if not greatness, move down this path?

Market selection is the decision to focus, to be specialized, and to risk the loss of the mundane to achieve the meaningful. It's the decision to shrink to a firm of 15, to allow yourself to grow to a firm of 100. It's the confidence that says that depth of knowledge is extraordinarily valuable to those in the place we blithely refer to as a market. In short, market selection is a marriage, a marriage of talent with need, and even if it sometimes seems as if one isn't seeking the other, they are in fact always on the prowl. The markets—or, more accurately, the clients—are actually more inwardly focused than we imagine. They are dealing with their own constraints, their own politics, and their own stifling bureaucratic practices. Can a design firm that deeply understands and cares about these and other issues actually make a difference?

From the client perspective, they want to be both understood and coveted. Whether the project is a set of fairly standard municipal buildings, a five-star resort, or the highest order of federal court facilities ever designed, the clients in question expect not only to receive professional performance and quality projects, they also expect to be led. They desire to collaborate with firms that can educate them on the latest concepts and innovations that will elevate their profile and make them more effective and efficient. Clients are willing to listen to those who are ahead of them, who are in tune with them, and who are committed to the vicissitudes of their particular environment. Can a design firm that commits to this level of concern about a unique client set succeed in winning these jobs in good times and in times of economic uncertainty? The answer is affirmative, and without reservation.

Winning influence with clients is a matter of patience and persistence. When a client looks at a firm's website or reads an article in the local paper, what is the lasting impression? If a hotelier is tracking a specialist in hospitality design, there is an expectation of learning a competitive secret that a generalist firm cannot deliver. If a generalist firm touts a hotel project, that same client will take notice, but will also begin to research other firms whose credentials are deeper and show more innovation, reflecting a greater commitment to their industry. The patience required to succeed comes from the decision to be focused on a particular market or two that the firm has an affinity for. The persistence comes from the understanding that the firm must digest every valuable piece of information about the target industry and place it in the overall context of their strategy and positioning effort. As these forces grow with time, the confidence of the firm takes on a life of its own, and is reflected in credibility that only comes with the decision to remain focused.

Market focus requires patience, and, likewise, market penetration and influence require persistence. These qualities cannot be replaced by the twists and turns firms commonly engage in when attempting to work for clients in markets they don't know and won't care to know once the project is completed.

CASE STUDY: JOHN MIOLOGOS, AIA, CIS, WEIGHS IN ON MARKET FOCUS AND SPECIALIZATION

CONNECTING EDUCATION, EXPERIENCE, AND MARKET POSITIONING

John Miologos, executive vice president for architecture, engineering, and construction management for WD Partners in Columbus, Ohio, gets right to the point when the topic of architectural firm specialization comes up: "My strongest desire is to be a catalyst to help the architectural profession understand that specialization will advance the industry." John's belief in this essential tenet for architectural firms is grounded in his long track record working "inside" a major client company. He feels that the experience and perspective gained from that tenure have allowed him to become a more accomplished resource for his clients, well beyond the skills obtained from his technical training.

As they bring architects in-house, construction management firms, engineering firms, and real estate development companies continue to encroach on what has been the traditional territory of architectural firms. John sees great opportunity to reverse this trend. Without discounting the value of design as a skill and a service, he adds, "It's a matter of being more client-centric, and perhaps not as design-centric. After years of working within an industry, I can bring a great deal of knowledge to bear about my client's needs that goes beyond simply designing a building. I understand what their competitors are doing, and the costs benchmarks on their spaces. I know the consumer trends that are shaping the way they should be going to market. I understand what is important to their customers when they are shopping in their stores, as well as the latest technology, materials, and building methods that are being used. It's clear time and again that I'm able to take them to the next level, and not only offer them ideas that demonstrate that I understand their business, but help them become more competitive and profitable. For example, I was recently able to help a client determine how to better allocate the money budgeted to refresh their stores. She originally wanted to spend the bulk of the budget on interior changes. However, through our discussions, I counseled her to spend more of their dollars for exterior improvements, because people often have to see evidence of a change on the outside of a building first before they will come inside the store so that the retailer can get 'credit' for interior changes."

Miologos's client-focused perspective can offer true innovation through collaboration with other interdisciplinary team members. He works with experts from a range of roles and functions such as market analysis; consumer research; product development; branding strategies; operations; mechanical, structural, and civil engineering; and real estate. And in the recent economic climate, his clients also ask for assistance with reducing capital expenditures and controlling costs.

"I truly believe that the architectural industry needs to let go of the generalist approach to running a design firm. The world has become much too complex for a client to expect that a firm with little experience in their industry is going to bring the types of innovation and ideas needed to position them in highly competitive markets." On why there continues to be resistance within the design industry, John suggests that, like a lot of change in life, it's a matter of time and effort. And to be honest, architects are struggling against the change in their relative professional status, as projects become more team-oriented. The architect is now an orchestra member, rather than the maestro.

Once practitioners take the leap, however, he suggests their point of view will shift rapidly. "Specialization has developed fairly significantly within the health care and education markets," according to John. "These industries understand their success comes with specialization, and they want to work with experts when it comes to architectural services. Also, more architectural schools are beginning to offer specialized learning in these fields, so that helps tremendously. I'd just like to see more offerings for additional areas of study that can bolster this need for market-specific knowledge." Committing to deeper market expertise will require practitioners to look across greater geographic territories to find new projects, but John sees that today's generation is ready to travel, if that's what it takes.

When it comes to advice for how to head down this path, John offers a nontraditional approach to planning a design career. "Go to a school that offers a more specialized program so you can learn about an industry, not just how to become an architect. Join a firm that has that focus, get your feet wet, and then go to work for a client for a few years. Once you've seen their world from the inside, go back to the world of design consultancy, and you'll be much better equipped and more valuable as a consultant."

Although John spent the majority of his career inside a client firm, he doesn't think that's a necessity to gain the value of the experience. Spending up to five years there will provide a substantial amount of exposure to give the architect a more specialized set of skills and perspective on how architecture "fits" in the business. On this point, John is adamant, saying, "These experiences can't be found through the standard educational experience. The client world is the real world, and we as an industry need to keep finding new ways to get closer to the companies and organizations we serve. There is no

> turning back from the specialization trend, so we need to work harder to make it happen for the design industry as a whole."
>
> Take the time, find the path, and make the effort if you agree with John that the design industry has much to gain by specialization.

As a postscript to the subject of specialization, it's not always the number of markets that a firm takes on that makes the difference. It's how a firm designs an approach that breeds and nourishes specialization that makes the distinction a reality. In addition to the following brief discussion, Chapter 5, "The Marketing System," explores this concept from other angles.

POSITIONING WITHIN MULTIPLE MARKETS

If a firm desires to serve multiple markets, it's very likely that each of those markets will require a different approach to marketing, project execution, and client relations. The classic example is public versus private clients. Working with the fastest-growing chain of bistro-style restaurants doesn't blend well with the pursuit of the next federal courthouse project. Yet many firms make this inherent conflict evident on their websites as they display their previous work. The problem arises when a firm doesn't manage itself within the appropriate rules and boundaries of the business model that best applies. The challenge of attracting diverse types of clients cannot be met by making small tweaks to proposals, and the larger tweaks begin to move the firm in different directions that often mean significant changes to positioning and operational aspects. Moving staff around to work on a variety of jobs is fine for experience and exposure, but not establishing a clear set of rules for managing vastly different client expectations and needs can undermine an otherwise good project.

To mitigate and manage these problems, consider the following procedures:

- Ensure that every project taken on is clearly slotted within one of the six archetypal operating models discussed in Chapter 3, and detailed in the appendix of this book.
- Develop sub-branding strategies and positioning plans that bring individual studio and practice group leaders to the fore with clients. This personification of a distinct and dedicated team within the larger firm goes a long way toward fostering the knowledge and skills necessary to compete with other specialized firms.

- If the firm has fewer than 100 staff members, try to limit the number of operating models in effect to two. For example, if you've historically been a Community Leader firm, and you want to develop more of a niche specialty in senior housing, make sure that each piece of the business develops its own strategy and rules for operating. Consider qualifying staff members for each market type, and be sure to segregate marketing functions, design standards, and quality control aspects.

- Consider the development of different websites along with other marketing materials, if the range of client types is significant. Without this approach, a firm's website begins to look like a huge compromise that's trying to please everyone at once, ultimately satisfying no one. When this happens, many firms turn their marketing attention on themselves by overemphasizing their list of core services and capabilities. This typically leads to further commoditization within the marketplace, since the firm is unable to take a stronger position based on more substantive achievements that come with a dedication to specific markets.

- For a larger firm with deep portfolios in many markets, there's still a need to reassess its true commitment to each market, even if it's operating within a profit-centered, divisional-style organization. Unless a firm is aggressive in managing its focus and expertise, markets can shift from vibrant and compelling into mundane and shrinking. As this occurs in a large firm, unhealthy internal competitiveness and resource allocation disagreements can begin to tear the firm apart. The assumption that a previous bread-and-butter market will bounce back can ultimately damage a reputation and force out the talent that's needed to turn the situation around. Again, a clear sub-branding positioning plan can avert these difficulties by creating strong identities under the already recognized firm umbrella.

The bottom line is that every firm, regardless of the number of markets it chooses to serve, needs to do so deliberately and with a focus and commitment that clients interpret as concentrated on their needs. Leaders who understand the nature of unwitting compromise and the drift from clear commitment to "trying their best" know that there's a large price to pay for taking on a project simply because it's available. The best leaders understand that the biggest project right around the block isn't worth 10 minutes' consideration, much less a proposal, if it doesn't fit the firm's identity and the way they function. As in the world of athletics, very few can perform at the highest levels of more than one sport. As the design industry continues to change, this aspect will emerge as the most important decision that a firm should make in order to thrive in the new world order.

THE CONVERGENCE OF IDEAS ESSENTIAL FOR THE DESIGN INDUSTRY

Although sustainability has been the headline for the past number of years, the less exciting but perhaps equally valuable approach to project execution represented by Integrated Project Delivery (IPD) continues to move forward. Supported by the development of Building Information Modeling (BIM), IPD is likely to gain in standing as the design industry reevaluates its prospects for the future. With a clear need to foster stronger project teams and work more efficiently, the design and construction industries will be compelled to work more closely to set and meet common goals in the interests of the clients. Too many firms are still offering only watered-down versions of both of these important tools, but the firms that will reap the emerging opportunities are working overtime to develop advanced systems and organizations that will propel the design industry to higher levels of achievement.

CASE STUDY: LPA IS MAKING THE CASE FOR INTEGRATED SUSTAINABLE DESIGN

It doesn't take long for Dan Heinfeld, president of Irvine, California–based LPA, Inc. to get to the point when the topic of sustainability comes up. With the vocal intonations of someone clearly on a mission, he says: "The whole idea of creating a truly sustainable project isn't just about filling out a score card. It's really about making sustainability integrated into the building so that it literally becomes part of the building's DNA." When the USGBC introduced its rating system for energy-efficient, high-performance buildings, architects, engineers, and other design professionals were among its first proponents, and LPA took an early lead in embracing the new rating system. The architectural firm designed Orange County's first LEED and LEED Platinum projects: the Premier Automotive Group building in Irvine and the Environmental Nature Center in Newport Beach.

In 2003, LPA set a goal of having its entire professional staff be LEED-accredited, according to Heinfeld. So far, 140 LPA professionals constituting 70 percent of the staff, including the firm's offices in Roseville and San Diego, have earned the credential.

"We wanted to show to our clients in the industry that we believe sustainable building needs to be a cultural thing within an office," Heinfeld said. "And we wanted to have that expertise and knowledge widespread throughout the firm, and not be in the collective hands of two or three people." LPA provides all of the training in-house and pays for the testing. The training takes places from noon to 2:00 p.m. on Fridays, when the firm typically works a half-day.

LPA's approach reflects a different attitude compared to many of the firm's peers, which might have a director of sustainability or similar title. However, Heinfeld says that sustainable thinking needs to happen all through the development of the project, which is why everybody in the firm needs to have that knowledge and commitment. "We're committed to doing informed design," said Heinfeld, "and it's one of the big reasons we've established LPA University." LPA U is a monthly program that focuses on an aspect of sustainability such as natural ventilation, green roofs, solar energy, and so forth. The sessions are taped so that people who missed them can look them up later online. All sessions are AIA CLU units and will also be part of the LEED Continuing Education. AIA has over 50 different Continuing Education opportunities on average in a year for staff, and they have a great deal of variety, including the Toastmasters and mock interviews for license candidates, as well as lessons learned programs.

Illustrating how much more sustainable the firm's projects are today than they would have been two or three years ago, Heinfeld noted that LPA currently has 10 projects that have LEED certification, and another 45 projects in design or seeking LEED certification. That number shows the growth of sustainability and the firm's approach to a Mainstream Green. "We're finding ways to create greener, more affordable sustainable projects all the time because of that knowledge," Heinfeld said.

The LPA View on Integrated Sustainable Design

A strong vision and recognition of the importance of brand development are keys to the advancement of ambitious firms. The following statement is written from the perspective of LPA, Inc., and represents the essence of their thinking about Integrated Sustainable Design.

The traditional practice of separate disciplines that are cobbled together for a project is not a sustainable model for the architectural profession in the future. LPA is looking to create a very different kind of design firm where in-house disciplines of architecture, interiors, landscape, and engineering are all working in balance, in search of appropriate and real sustainable solutions.

An Integrated Sustainable Design process promotes input from a variety of stakeholders that profoundly changes the design process and therefore the design outcome. Our firm is a 45-year-old practice that started this integrated process over 20 years ago when we brought landscape architecture in-house. Over the years, we added interior design, graphics, and furniture services. Starting three years ago with the purchase of a structural engineering firm, LPA became a full-service A & E design firm, now offering engineering disciplines of civil, structural, mechanical, plumbing, and electrical. We have changed the traditional practice of "hiring" consultants to a "partnership" that focuses on "integrated sustainable design." We challenge our integrated teams to find holistic, affordable, and sustainable solutions for each project, using a multidisciplined collaborative approach whereby design is "informed" by the collective knowledge of the team. There are a number of A & E firms in the country, but rarely are they in balance whereby the quality of the architecture and engineering are equally excellent. We believe that sustainability can inform our company to create a firm where the architects learn from the engineers and the engineers learn from the architects to shape a group of professionals with one purpose: to make sustainability MAINSTREAM. That means every building, regardless of budget or program, has a sustainable quotient. Our sustainable future depends on it.

The other principle that is leading the firm to embrace and foster this integrated approach is our belief that design excellence and sustainability are part of the same process, and we have therefore created a collaborative environment for all stakeholders to contribute in the design effort.

In order to create real integration between architects and engineers, we knew that we needed to make the collaboration happen literally in the hallways and at improvised meetings, so that the interaction would occur often, with the intent of building on success. The more the teams met and worked together, the better the communication and the shared knowledge. We knew from experience that real integration doesn't happen at planned meetings or consultant reviews, but from everyday connections and an ongoing exposure to each other; therefore, we have added engineering services to LPA's services profile. Some of the benefits of having in-house engineering that we did not originally plan on or think about, but that have been quite valuable to the firm, follow:

- Peer Review: We have a goal of reaching 80 percent LPA engineering on our projects. While this goal will take time to achieve, we are working with a number of outside engineering firms and always will. Having the in-house engineers do peer reviews—setting standards, checking proposals, and reviewing all of LPA's projects—has been very helpful to the firm in establishing a consistent quality and brand.

- BIM/Revit: Having our engineers working on the same BIM models in real time as part of the design team has been very valuable in the process and in helping us to fully integrate and bring BIM into the firm.

- In these difficult economic times and with a slow recovery predicted, our firm will not only be able to control cash flow better, but we will also have the opportunity to grow our engineering services and the firm.

Our multidisciplined teams are looking to solve problems that are facing our clients while not chasing fashion: the results are a regionally appropriate and timeless beauty. This holistic approach has led our teams to create some of the landmark projects in the sustainable movement:

- The largest LEED Gold office building in the country at the time of its completion: the 660,000-sq.-ft. Toyota South Campus. This project has been credited by USGBC president Rick Fedrizzi with busting the myth that sustainability adds cost to a project.

- The first LEED NC project in the country: the 330,000-sq.-ft. Premier Automotive Group Headquarters.

- The first LEED-rated project for the Jet Propulsion Lab in Pasadena and the greenest facility in the entire NASA family, the LEED Gold 200,000-sq.-ft. Flight Centers Project.

Dan Heinfeld is completely convinced that becoming an A & E firm committed to sustainable design is the best decision LPA has ever made. "We have an integrated delivery process, it's easier for our clients, and we create better buildings. And quite importantly, it gives us the ability to grow in a down market. Those four reasons are too powerful to choose any other path."

GEOGRAPHIC REACH AND POSITIONING

Geographic reach for design firms is a multifaceted aspect of strategy and positioning that deserves closer scrutiny as a firm is defining its place in the world. Many architects are willing to take projects in any locale, yet most do not actively pursue new work outside their traditionally defined comfort zone. Engineers are similar in this regard, except for the preponderance of civil firms that tend to cluster in a more regional fashion. As a baseline, firms can be seen as local, regional, national, or international in scope. Implications for these choices are numerous and have a strong influence on how far a firm can go in terms of depth of specialization within markets and project types.

Management and organizational control challenges are a significant part of the equation to consider when reaching for new territory, and many firms that attempt expansion can be unprepared for this change in their operational and marketing functions. Regardless, it is likely that the future of the design industry will have fewer firms with an overall greater reach as the economic system is recalibrated over the next decade. With lower growth prospects, successful firms will encroach on the geography of weaker firms, and through advances in technology and communication, will change the landscape of the industry for the foreseeable future.

Primary Reasons for Geographic Expansion:

- An existing client takes the firm to a new location.
- Talent is available to start a new office.
- Merger and acquisition activity takes place.
- The firm pursues a specific project type.
- The firm adopts a broad positioning strategy for its market focus.

Moving beyond Local

A local firm has two primary choices when desiring a larger geographic footprint: either reproduce itself as a local firm in a new location, or change its business model to move toward a regional or national status. For many engineering firms, the replication approach is more comfortable because of the depth of local knowledge and connections required to succeed in any city or county environment. As a Community Leader, such an engineering firm would find the change to a Niche Expert model too dramatic a shift to accomplish successfully. Architects with a historical local presence can make this shift more readily, yet must also be ready to market under a new set of rules, travel more regularly, and begin to turn down "easy" projects that show up on their doorstep because of their familiar local profile. Another choice for a local firm seeking broader geography is to hook up with a large national firm that is looking for local support. If the firm begins to build its experience level on higher-profile projects, this can translate into a more competitive resume down the road. As with many shifts in scope, the biggest obstacle to overcome is one of mindset. A firm must adjust how it sees itself before the market will embrace a new story or accept the promise of effective performance from an out-of-town provider.

Figure 4.1 shows the steps of a local to regional decision model. Such a decision model is required for any serious attempt to transform the firm's

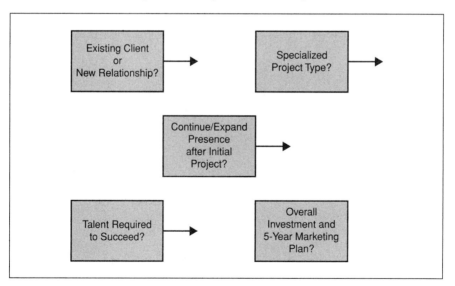

Figure 4.1 Moving from a tradition as a local firm to creating a regional presence typically requires a more specialized market focus. It also often means finding new talent to add to the staff who have "been there before." (*Source:* SPARKS, The Center for Strategic Planning)

geography. The mindset issue can be problematic when firms "back into" out-of-town opportunities they are fully capable of performing, but haven't comprehended specifically what it means to build a new presence in unfamiliar territory. Leaders should ask themselves three critical questions before promoting themselves to a wider audience:

- Are we prepared to deepen our focus on the market or project type represented by this opportunity?
- Is the project manager team ready to commit to solving the issues connected to distance and remote client relations?
- Will the status of this project significantly increase our level of recognition upon successful completion?

The answers to these questions form the basis for seeing the individual project as a one-shot opportunity versus the beginning of a larger quest for growth beyond current borders.

Going National

Moving from regional to national status in the design industry involves a different set of decisions and considerations. Regional geographic coverage is reasonably safe in terms of the issues of travel and commitment to a niche project type. When a firm decides to become national in scope, the stakes become higher and fraught with systemic organizational considerations. A decision model for moving from regional to national status includes the questions posed in Figure 4.2.

Becoming a nationally recognized firm involves a level of commitment that only a minority of firms can achieve. National recognition requires a certainty of purpose plus a clear alignment with a project type that is bound to become part of the fabric of American existence. In short, when firms become nationally known Niche Experts, they are aligning themselves with a significant aspect of current social experience. It's one thing to nurture a firm along with a set of clients that may or may not break through to influence social or economic norms—it's quite another to be at the helm of a firm that has determined that they are the force that will define those norms for the succeeding generations.

The role of a Niche Expert is in fact to be the leading influence on our society's gathering places. These firms determine the setting and the tone, and they design the look and the feel of the spaces where we gather to give and receive the gifts that our epoch determines are of greatest value. Given the magnitude of importance of this role, the questions posed by the decision model must be answered before a firm attempts to aspire to this level of influence.

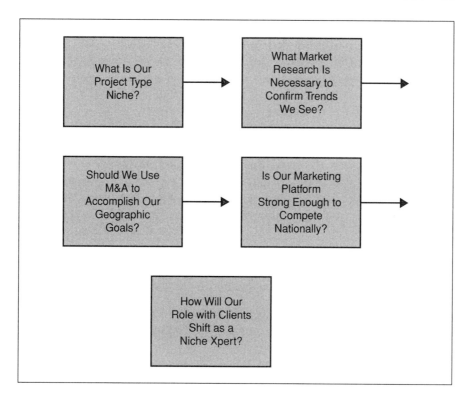

Figure 4.2 Becoming a national firm requires strong project specialization and market expertise. While M&A is often used to accomplish this step, there are numerous complications and pitfalls to consider carefully. (*Source:* SPARKS, The Center for Strategic Planning)

A firm that knows and understands its niche on a wide geographic scale has the opportunity to create generational memories. It studies its market carefully, knows the trends that underlie the essential desires of the constituents, and has faith in its ability to market and promote the final outcome. On a business level, this firm is relentless in its determination to perfect its image and reputation for delivering a highly lauded product, and fully expects to receive both the artistic accolades and the financial rewards associated with its efforts. In short, a nationally recognized Niche Expert firm can go anywhere it chooses. Its marketing effort actually decreases as time goes on, as it achieves a oneness with its name and its work that no marketing program can exceed. Market selection isn't a matter of defensive positioning against a possible economic downturn. It is a matter of passion and determination, designed to make a commitment to a core set of beliefs about the value that can be derived from the firm's unique set of skills and perspectives as designers—a collection of talents that cannot be replaced by technology or any other incremental advance advocated as the next solution to our pressing needs.

CASE STUDY: GEOGRAPHIC EXPANSION IN A SHIFTING GLOBAL ECONOMY

Brian Lewis knew that the economic turmoil of 2009 created a problem he had to solve. As the practice manager and senior principal of a Trinidad firm started in 1944, he recognized that the days of plentiful projects were clearly in the rearview mirror, at least for the time being. As a firm of 18 in total staff size, acla:works was considered a strong player in the markets of Port of Spain and other Trinidad locales. His firm had been responsible for the design of many iconic structures, a list including Republic Bank, the Halls of Justice, the Ministry of Public Administration and Information Building, the Financial Complex, and the Institute of Marine Affairs. He also spearheaded the use of BIM on the firm's projects as early as 2005, leveraging the firm to become the leading proponent within the Caribbean. The oil and gas riches of the region had been good for everyone over the years, but the global slowdown was hitting this country of 1.3 million people very hard. In addition to the credit crunch and banking crisis, the government had taken to giving more projects to nonlocal firms, making the squeeze even worse.

By the summer of 2009, Brian's wheels were turning faster. Along with the three other directors of the firm, he envisioned a deliberate and comprehensive outreach to a number of Caribbean islands to the north, in search of new partnerships, new clients, and most certainly, new work. As Gary Turton, head of marketing, recalls, "We developed this vision of a network of firms that our firm could lead and develop across a number of islands. In times like these, creative approaches are demanded, and we were determined to make this a viable solution for our firm." With a half-dozen supporting subconsultant firms on the team, representing service providers in Trinidad who had worked with acla:works in the past, they were ready to launch. Their first step was a three-day strategy session to hammer out ideas and hand out initial assignments. The decision was made to base the new consortium operation in Barbados, since Brian was born there and it had the right financial infrastructure to meet the group's needs. Within weeks, a trip to Barbados had yielded a small truckload of contacts and possibilities. A branch office was established, and through numerous lunches and meetings, the network began to take shape, interviewing as many as 10 architectural practices in Barbados.

From a markets perspective, the Caribbean Outreach program is going to be across the board: corporate, institutional, urban planning, resorts, housing. Governments up and down the chain of islands have large numbers of projects on hold, so the team is working hard to discover any financing opportunities that can be the impetus to resurrect stalled work. On the private side, the financial and tourism sectors are moving at a snail's pace, but the team remains confident they will begin to move again soon.

In terms of the firm's overall identity, the strategy session brought a few important points to light. Peter Chandler, acla:works director, explains: "We operate as a community leader here in Trinidad, which is logical due to the relatively small size of the market as an island country. We thought that may be a weakness as we moved towards other Caribbean opportunities, but we've found that's exactly the approach that works in those other locales as well."

Survive and Thrive

When considering the realities at hand of economic turmoil and unfavorable local government policy, one of the key discussions held during the strategy session was "Survive and Thrive." It had already been determined that limited market focus per se was off the table for consideration—times were too tough to narrow things down. And it was clear that the firm still needed some government work for cash flow purposes, and to keep themselves in favorable standing for when things got better. This is where acla:works' expertise in BIM began to make a big difference: It was decided to use the BIM story as a key marketing tool both at home and farther north. According to Junior Thompson, director at acla:works, "We had worked very hard for three years on making BIM a major force for the firm, and we felt it could be an important part of this strategy." From the new ideas angle, it was also decided that the sustainability mentality was ready to take hold in the greater Caribbean. Lastly, a new interiors focus could help keep previous clients on the radar screen and generate new client contacts as time went by.

The elements of the Survive and Thrive campaign are shown in Figure 4.3. The line depicting the split between BIM and sustainability shouldn't be taken as a divide. BIM and sustainability are valid and important drivers and tools on either side of the equation; however, BIM is seen as a more powerful topic to attract government work at this time. In addition to the government versus private client positioning, it was deemed important that the firm pursue design-build contractors, particularly for work in Trinidad. Consortium work "up the islands" is likely going to be more CM-based.

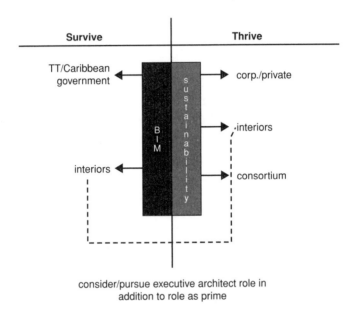

consider/pursue executive architect role in
addition to role as prime

Figure 4.3 In this example, the firm is seeking to balance their profile in their local market with a new initiative to expand to new Caribbean locations. (*Source:* acla:works)

BIM

The firm is understandably proud of their accomplishments with BIM, and the overall strategy is articulated as follows:

"Whether it be within Trinidad, working with design-build contractors, or looking to enter other Caribbean markets, the BIM strengths of acla:works will play a significant role. The firm has run a Trinidad and Tobago seminar with Martin Fischer of Stanford with good results, and may want to use his commentary and thoughts as a marketing lever. He may agree to record a short video or offer key quotations that would support the firm's objectives.

"The firm should strongly consider creating a variety of versions for our BIM story. One version for contractors, one for government

(Trinidad & Tobago), and one for other Caribbean government entities would be advisable.

"When we sat around the office discussing the BIM equation, we decided to come up with the dreaded list of repetitive questions that all architects and consultants wrestle with on every project. Those key questions should be asked and answered in BIM-talk as part of the presentation. From our experience, these questions are typically:

- How to minimize the cost of changes?
- How to get better cost controls, less project delay?
- How can we eliminate coordination errors and sequencing problems?
- How to ensure/measure contractor performance?
- Can the client get a complete set of accurate fully coordinated error-free drawings?
- How to avoid conflicts of services? (Pipes into beams)
- Additional topics for questions to be answered: quality control, risk, client expectations, visualization, cash flow, energy efficiencies, schedule performance, approvals, etc.

"As we discussed a number of times in our planning session, the BIM topic is terrific to break the ice with a new client, a new island or a new constituency. We've developed a powerful PowerPoint presentation of the firm's profile that includes the benefits of using BIM with a number of animated examples that are quite compelling. The BIM program will be positioned as an educational effort— non-threatening, the sharing of important information—allowing those in attendance to explore the technology and its effects on projects without the pressures of shortlists or the final selection of the consulting team for a specific project."

Taken from the memorandum of understanding (MOU) the firm has developed for its new positioning effort, here are the mission and vision of the overall program:

> The mission of acla:works is to be the prominent architecture firm in the Caribbean by 2020 in terms of image, perception, service level and delivery. Its business plan is to expand outward into the Caribbean to capture business opportunities through strategic initiatives, local joint ventures, and networking collaborations.

Within the plan are the following objectives:

1. Expand the acla:works brand
2. Develop a marketing network
3. Provide the highest-quality design, service, and tools [BIM, LEED, IPD]
4. Collaborate with strategically selected design partners
5. Expand design and support resources to compete to undertake larger projects
6. Create a pool of specialized design services

The first phase of our mission is to open branch offices in strategic Caribbean countries and then to formalize working relationships with carefully selected local architectural firms. Branch offices shall be responsible for accounting, administration and marketing but will not actually be commissioned for professional services.

acla:works may develop a license for the use of certain branding tools that may be available and could include [for instance] marketing tools, software training, office management software systems, financial planning tools, design and project management software training, building information modeling systems, integrated project delivery, design-build, etc. The intention here is to ensure strategic partner firms develop certain skills that will promote greater inter-office collaboration and expand resource capability.

While still a work in progress, the Caribbean Outreach program is moving along at full speed. With five months of effort under their belt, the numbers are impressive. After four trips to Barbados, they've generated over 100 contacts, established a branch office, identified three job prospects, and acquired 17 new leads. They have also produced a 30-page brochure of the firm's work, and are getting ready to revamp the website to make it more interactive and dynamic.

The team is ready to move on to St. Lucia next, and continue to spread the word about their capabilities, tools, and ideas for getting important projects accomplished in a time when many firms find themselves uncertain of which way to turn.

—(Author's note: In November 2009, acla:works published a book about its founder titled *Manikin: The Art & Architecture of Anthony C. Lewis.*)

As another example of market growth through geographic expansion, SMRT has taken a measured approach within the Northeast, culminating in a number of significant successes. The new GE Healthcare facility in the Albany, New York, area is their most recent major achievement to bear fruit from this initiative.

CASE STUDY: SMRT, PORTLAND, MAINE

STILL FLEXIBLE AFTER 126 YEARS: A SMALL-CITY FIRM EXPANDS IN A BIG WAY

As the fourth-generation Stevens to be at the helm of SMRT, an 80-person firm in Portland, Maine, Paul Stevens is proud and excited when the conversation turns to some of the more notable projects his firm has taken on. The firm is also an early adopter of Integrated Project Delivery, and he speaks convincingly about how SMRT's success with design-build is really an attitude—a different way of thinking, with the contractor seen as a full teammate. But as the product of over 25 years of design-build effort, he particularly enjoys retracing the earlier days of getting into the science and technology market. Originally, the SMRT engineering group focused on supporting the architectural projects: the schools, commercial buildings, municipal facilities, and a small amount of healthcare work. However, they found it difficult to maintain a steady workflow for the engineers. Under Paul's guidance, the firm made a strategic decision to develop the capability to execute challenging engineering-led projects, in order to attract better talent and smooth out the workload. They recruited the lead facility engineer from a local semiconductor manufacturer as the firm's chief engineer, charging him to develop that new strategic business. As it turns out, the strategy worked very well. They broke into engineering design for high-tech projects, and enhanced their ability to serve their healthcare clients.

And while the firm was still very comfortable within its Portland roots, Paul made another important decision in 2003 that led to major projects that reach world-class status. As he explains: "We knew we needed to broaden our geography somewhat if we wanted to keep our high-tech and science practice vital. So, in 2003 we hired a marketing consultant, Phillippe Trotin, to research opportunities in other northeastern geographic areas since Maine and New Hampshire were fairly limited in that client type. The Albany, NY, area stood out due to the incentives to industry being offered by New York State, the concentration of academic institutions and the small number of A/E firms in the area doing this type of work. We decided to explore the possibilities further and put our marketing consultant on the ground on a part-time basis to make contacts and verify our initial findings. Good prospects were uncovered and in early 2004 we leased a small office in Troy as a place to work and as a place to meet with people. We had no permanent staff, but Dick Bilodeau, our senior engineer, and I spent time there on a regular basis. The initial small projects we were able to land were produced in our Maine office. In addition to the high-tech work, we discovered that there was good opportunity in another of our specialties, correctional work, which I also began marketing actively. This resulted in a significant new county jail project in St. Lawrence County a couple of years ago."

By late 2004, SMRT had a large enough book of work to move a senior mechanical engineer (also an owner of the firm) from Maine to be in the Albany area office full time. Russ Bailey had been with SMRT for a number of years and had been senior engineer and project manager for many of the high-tech projects. Russ was a good fit because he could do the engineering work as well as manage the start-up. In addition to prime contract opportunities, they also marketed their engineering services to local architects to help support the office. This strategy continues today, but they are also working to become less dependent on this work in the coming year.

Paul laughs when he's asked how such a long-established firm continues to reinvent itself. "I've always realized that flexibility in our approach serves us well from a strategy standpoint. Frankly, we make our decisions, hold to them, and it seems one thing leads us to another, and so on."

It was in 2007 that the firm got its first big break, winning the award for the design of a new 230,000-sq.-ft., $130,000,000 clean manufacturing facility. This award was the result of a combination of factors: (1) SMRT had the expertise, and in particular Dick Bilodeau's experience working as a facility engineer in clean manufacturing facilities, (2) they were established with their Albany office presence, and (3) they had a longtime relationship with Blake Hodess of

Hodess Construction Corporation, with whom they executed their first design-build project many years ago. Although he was not the prime CM on the project, Hodess was subcontracted to Turner Construction for the construction of the clean rooms. It was through the Hodess connections that SMRT was able to be considered for the job. Dick Bilodeau, the senior mechanical engineer, came to SMRT from National Semiconductor 20 years ago and established SMRT's high-tech engineering group. His facilities background enables him to be very effective in helping companies with pre-planning and detailed planning early in the process. This was the initial work that he was doing with the client, and his success in that phase enabled the firm to be selected as prime engineers when the project advanced from planning to reality. Also, this project was awarded a LEED Gold certification—very difficult to achieve for this type of facility, as a result of enormous energy demands.

Other evolutionary changes continue for SMRT as this regional expansion takes hold. In 2008, they hired Scott Goodwill as office director, freeing up Russ Bailey to concentrate more on the engineering side of the equation. Scott came to them from a senior mechanical engineering position at EYP's Albany office. That same year, they moved from the small space in Troy to a larger office in Latham, near the airport. They now have a staff of seven in the office and are actively recruiting additional talent. For 2010, they are also expanding their healthcare marketing into upstate New York. Steady development of that market focus has just resulted in the award of a $225 million stand-alone hospital project that has Paul Stevens very excited. "I'm delighted at the progress we've been able to make from our unique perch up here in Portland. Not being in the mix of a megalopolis may hold some firms back, but we've worked at changing things on our own terms."

Strategic engagement on the services level can be a strong source of growth in certain markets. A bioengineering firm in Massachusetts is accomplishing their long-term vision through a design-build strategy, along with a deep interdisciplinary approach.

CASE STUDY: BIOENGINEERING GROUP, SALEM, MASSACHUSETTS

SERVICE DELIVERY AS A KEY STRATEGY FOR FIRM GROWTH

During Bioengineering Group's first formal strategy retreat in 1999, the takeaway goal was growth. The staff, which numbered 12 at the time, looked at growth as a way to achieve greater impact in building sustainable communities, the founding vision for the company. They also saw that the pathway to success was to create a unique position in the marketplace through a more innovative and influential service delivery approach.

CEO Wendi Goldsmith, who started the firm in Salem, Massachusetts, in 1992 at the age of 26, believed from the start that her firm could adopt a vastly different business model than the companies she worked for early in her career.

"What I noticed was how risk averse the culture of technical and engineering firms was, particularly in developing solutions for clients," Goldsmith said. "Innovation was compromised by fear of doing the wrong thing. Even when there was technical merit to a new approach or idea, a cultural aversion to risk got between the idea and its adoption."

"What if the client doesn't like the idea?" was a recurring theme. "Is there any chance this could make waves and be portrayed by someone as a mistake?" The result of this apprehension, according to Goldsmith, was a predictable repetition in project delivery. "Taking the well-traveled path and cranking out the same prescriptive solutions was the security blanket no one was willing to give up."

She knew it could be much different—and consequently much better for clients. Goldsmith had the opportunity in her twenties to work overseas in Germany with a smart, leading-edge engineering firm recognized globally for their river restoration expertise. The team she worked with had a 25-year track record of providing creativity and sustainability on complex projects with major contamination, hydraulic, ecological, and historic issues. She got to experience what happened when innovation was applied to a big problem. It was a lesson she applied with her staff and clients at Bioengineering Group.

Today, the interdisciplinary firm of 75 is working on technically challenging and ecologically promising projects across the country. This includes the largest civil works project ever awarded in the U.S., the $1.3 billion Inner Harbor Navigation Canal (IHNC) barrier to protect greater New Orleans from hurricane surges. The company doubled in staff and revenue in 2009, earning an international award for fast growth and a Gold Medal for Business Achievement from the Environmental Business Journal.

In order to reach these ambitious goals for growth and differentiation in the marketplace, the firm needed two distinct engines: (1) applying an interdisciplinary model that defies industry conventions, and (2) developing design-build expertise well timed to the marketplace. To appreciate how the firm built these core growth engines requires a closer look under the hood.

Design-Build Breakthrough

Goldsmith's comfort level in taking on risk, combined with her belief in the power of exploring alternative solutions, put the firm in a position to comfortably test new ideas. A 1998 call from an executive at a private utility company with an urgent problem to solve resulted in the firm's first design-build project. A major gas distribution pipeline relocation was failing. Permitting problems caused by design and environmental impact threatened to shut down the pipeline. "Find someone who can do bioengineering" was the edict from state regulators. An Internet search located Bioengineering Group.

The project, completed under a fast-track, design-build approach, was a fantastic success. This experience led to winning other design-build projects, including critical environmental work on the $385 million Route 3 North highway widening, the first state design-build project in Massachusetts, plus an array of day-care facilities and stream and wetland restoration jobs for the U.S. Army Corps of Engineers. Success with design-build came about because the firm was able to continually build on the lessons learned from smaller projects and small-scale pilot projects performed in prior years. The marketplace also helped—a shift towards the design-build project delivery by federal and state clients came just as the experience curve at Bioengineering was in the right position.

On the coastal and riverway projects, where the firm had much of their experience, design-build works particularly well. "When you have a dynamic river system or coastal zone, the conditions below the waterline are constantly changing," Goldsmith said. "Design-build allows the team to be flexible and adapt the tasks to meet dynamic changes in ecology and terrain."

Interdisciplinary Advantage: Value Ecology from Day One

As design-build was creating growth opportunity, the internal organization and project approach methodology helped separate Bioengineering from the competition. The approach is based on providing as much value as feasible for the client.

From the early days of the firm to the present, the firm's approach has been to turn loose an eclectic team from across several disciplines and multiple backgrounds. A coastal restoration project, for example, might engage ecologists, earth scientists, botanists, engineers, and landscape design professionals working together to look at all aspects and test out ideas and solutions.

The model for many technical firms is to keep the project in the hands of the specialist team—engineers grouped for a civil project, or permitting specialists for gaining state and local regulatory approvals. Review by other disciplines in such a linear approach occurs only after the original planning and design are done, and to some degree after ownership of the work and the solution is staked out by those professionals responsible for that work.

"We can provide not only the expected for the client, but go far beyond the expected or the conventional by applying an interdisciplinary solution," said Goldsmith. "We set clear ecological goals from the project kickoff forward, then design to fulfill them along the way because of the rich variety of viewpoints and experiences on the team"

The Bioengineering Group approach, which is helping them keep and grow their client base, is one that stays closely in step with the major advances in computer modeling, GIS analysis, and other sophisticated tools that allow careful consideration of complex variables. Gone are the days when the design of a channel had to be based on slide-rule calculations—we now use tools that allow subtle changes in riverbank vegetation and geomorphic process to be accounted for in the engineering analysis, for instance. This approach is beneficial to clients because innovation can often come from the ecologists or earth scientists as much as the engineers or landscape architects, thus tapping a wider array of ideas. It also benefits the firm by creating a dynamic environment where professionals challenge, inspire, and educate one another.

When Wendi Goldsmith started the firm almost 20 years ago, she couldn't be sure where the business journey would take her. But she knew that the path to her core vision—building sustainable communities on an ecological foundation—would require a few risks to be taken and a few conventions to be tipped.

COMMODITIZATION OF DESIGN SERVICES

Much has been written and said regarding the commoditization of design services over the years. Key to the discussion is the way fees are frequently pounded down as a result of competition and the negotiation process. Many firms wind up keeping fees lower than the value of their services in order to stay afloat. However, that is the micro-view of the problem, and doesn't address the larger perspective on the issue. The macro-view is overall economic health and the consideration of business cycles. Next down the chain is market development, followed by firm development, which includes organizational strength, the development of services, and the quality of leadership. This section will review each of these considerations in that order, and explain how firms can better plan for the ultimate interplay of factors that frequently culminate in pressure on fees.

Economic Health and Business Cycles

Recent events in the global and U.S. economies have taught us all too well how it feels to be close to the edge of a very lofty cliff. Most businesses that rely on a sizable stream of credit and other sources of ready financing have suffered substantial declines in revenues and future prospects that make survival a real-time question. Some analyses have determined that this setback will take another 10 years to work its way through the system, as the system itself gets redesigned along the way.

Separate from the actual health of an economy is the reality of business cycles. After experiencing a decade of strong growth, many firms are complacent and begin to feel that even if there isn't continued growth, they will be able to maintain their recent level of revenues and profits. Everyone is busy, and the focus turns inward toward concerns such as career, stock ownership, and new technologies. Emerging markets and other newer opportunities are often overlooked, as it may seem to require too much effort to tackle that new situation when the traditional mix of clients is doing just fine.

Yet, as with the stock market, the reversal is looming just around the corner. In the U.S. economy, most recessions have been a function of inventory. Too much optimism leads to overcapacity and overproduction. Prices begin to be cut once the markets realize they've overshot their enthusiasm for the next leg of expansion, and the smallest cracks now become visibly larger. In a still healthy economic system, this type of slowdown will pass relatively quickly, and without significant lasting damage. Everyone breathes a sigh of relief, and continues down the same path that they've been on for years. With design and construction, the logical condition of leading during expansions and lagging during recovery creates a dislocation of expectations once the better times have already been booked.

From a long-term perspective, many firm owners simplify their thinking around this phenomenon by holding on to a reasonable-sounding belief that everything evens out over time. That may be the case for a 5–10 year period, but it isn't often the case for an entire career, and it's never the case when the underlying system breaks down. The usual strategies applied to managing through the weaker times are typically centered on cutting and controlling costs. Cheaper rent, cutbacks on marketing expenses, and a sudden fervor for internal efficiency that will boost profits in the short term are often the focus. Those are fine for the short run, but too often aren't sustained or thoroughly applied. They also are no match for a time interval when all the factors discussed here are working against you.

One point to consider that is often the defense against downward cycles is the public versus private market positioning. Many firms use government work as a countercyclical cushion when the private markets they serve weaken. On the surface, this makes sense, and perhaps one should always keep a hand in that till to help bridge a gap now and then. Larger issues loom, however, especially in relation to a firm's sense of itself, its willingness to invest deeply enough in the private markets it does serve, and the effect all these cumulative decisions have on the firm's image, reputation, and staff psyche. For firms that truly wish to serve the government markets, there are differences in marketing, pricing, contracts, operations, cash flow, and client relations that could fill a book, when compared to dealing with the private sector. Suffice it to say, the effect of these decisions is more significant than many firms are prepared for, both as a result of running to a new market out of fear and of letting their focus drift back, as recovery stabilizes. This dynamic is potentially disruptive to the positioning process, and can take a firm off track for many years.

Effective Fee Management Strategies

Fees are largely determined by the markets and clients firms serve. When a client represents a growing, vibrant market (or project type), the fees are logically higher when the service provider's focus matches the market's direction and needs. Secondarily, fees are affected by overall economic conditions, as previously noted, yet the dynamic shifts from one of pushing fee limits to hanging on when the business cycle turns against you. Many owners are strongly reluctant to decrease their fees, even in the face of deteriorating conditions. While this reaction is understandable to some degree, it's less than half the story. The real story related to fee strength is profitability, the end result of the equation. Are we choosing the right clients and projects, and are we managing these projects to maximize efficiency within the parameters of delivering a quality outcome? Questions along these lines are critical to maintaining the right perspective when it comes to a rationale for increasing or decreasing the firm's fees.

The most significant question becomes: "Are we able to make significant improvements to our internal operations in a way that delivers the right product, and pushes more profit to our bottom line?" Too many firms lament the external conditions, harp on competitors who are slashing fees, and yet don't take the time to focus on the types of improvements, beyond cost cutting, that could effectively make the topic moot. While there's no methodology to keep a competitor from taking a bath on a project, there are ways to increase your firm's strength. These actions can and should be taken in both good times and bad, and include the following:

- Detailed review of job descriptions and roles to ensure maximum efficiency, especially within the realm of project phase hand-offs and start/stop events that interrupt progress.
- Diligent reviews and internal training related to managing scope within the client's specifications.
- Charging for changes in scope that are client-driven/agreed upon.
- Development of stronger and more concise proposals that manage expectations, and contain terms and conditions that will allow for a healthy financial outcome.
- Relieving principals and project managers of tedious, inefficient, and wasteful uses of their time. Making copies, putting together overnight

packages, handling purely routine administrative issues, and many more mundane distractions contribute to potentially severe reductions in productivity and focus.

■ Improving communication within a team or a studio. Quite often, team members are uncertain of what's next, who's responsible, and how far they should proceed with their work.

These and many other elements of the workday, when not addressed, detract directly from the bottom line, and ultimately reduce the firm's flexibility to manage fees when external factors have taken over.

From a positioning standpoint, the relative strength and stability of a firm's fees can be an excellent indicator of how well (or poorly) the firm's leaders have prepared for the upside and weak side of cycles and trends. From a philosophical and supply-and-demand point of view, leaders should ask themselves questions centered on scarcity versus abundance. While it may be counterintuitive, being somewhat scarce in any market conditions might be a good strategy for a firm that is focused on taking on only the highest-quality engagements that match their strongest identity and purpose.

SERVICE DEVELOPMENT

In the world of professional services, with its project orientation and need to continually assess and manage risk, development of something akin to a "product" can be a real challenge. However, a product development mentality can be applied to services, and it should be, when a firm has their eyes on the positioning prize. Transforming a service into a product isn't exceedingly difficult on paper, but it takes great discipline and a creative mindset that understands how to add value to the fairly mundane tasks and processes many firms utilize in their daily operations.

The model in Figure 4.4 shows four very distinct levels of service to product development—the process of turning the invisible tasks performed in the execution of daily project work into a branded product that a firm can promote, own, and develop further as different project experiences are added to the mix.

Moving up the ladder towards the establishment of a better-defined service allows the firm to achieve better integration of the service into its project execution routine. This additional experience across the firm can bring about stories, additional improvements, and new applications that keep the service-as-product effort alive.

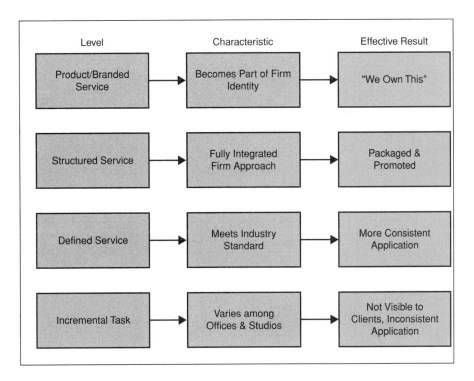

Level	Characteristic	Effective Result
Product/Branded Service	Becomes Part of Firm Identity	"We Own This"
Structured Service	Fully Integrated Firm Approach	Packaged & Promoted
Defined Service	Meets Industry Standard	More Consistent Application
Incremental Task	Varies among Offices & Studios	Not Visible to Clients, Inconsistent Application

Figure 4.4 Taking a product development approach to strengthening a firm's services can provide greater visibility and marketing power. It also offers branding opportunities that provide differentiation from the competition. (*Source:* SPARKS, The Center for Strategic Planning)

Walter P. Moore is large engineering firm based in Houston, Texas, with additional offices throughout the U.S. A few years ago, they developed and distributed a four-page brochure entitled *Seeing into the Building Envelope: Infrared Thermography Evaluates without Destruction.* Written by a PhD and a PE, the two pages of material inside the brochure provided a comprehensive summary of the service, describing the tool used and the application, as well as guidelines for best use of the tool. A brief case study was also referenced, in which more than 1,000 student housing units had been tested. Finally, two photos and two charts were included in the package, along with brief resumes of the two authors. From a series called *Moore Knowledge*, this marketing piece provides an excellent example of how to approach the "hardening" of a basic service into a product that the firm can promote and build a story around.

CHAPTER 5

THE MARKETING SYSTEM

ESTABLISHING A MARKETING SYSTEM MINDSET

Once a firm has established a clear identity and has generated a strategy-based positioning plan, development of their marketing system is crucial to ultimate positioning success. Critical to the approach devised to meet this challenge is the term "system," since it's only through a systems-oriented mindset that significant rewards can be achieved. As with many of the functions of a firm—such as human resources, project operations, or finance—the marketing function should be grounded in a set of beliefs and a philosophy that anchor it and become known throughout the organization. While many firms feel that the marketing process is working as long as they are able to sign new contracts with enough frequency, true marketing believers understand the additional depth of development required to create a strong marketing system. Such a system is sturdy, yet flexible enough to change to meet new challenges and opportunities. It's comprehensive but not burdensome, allowing for creativity to meet specialized needs without reinventing the entire structure. With these basic aspects in mind, let's consider the 10 elements shown in Figure 5.1, as the primary points for review and discussion.

As with other characteristics of positioning development, the marketing system should be created using both top-down thinking and bottom-up construction. Blending evidence of the big picture with the more task-driven,

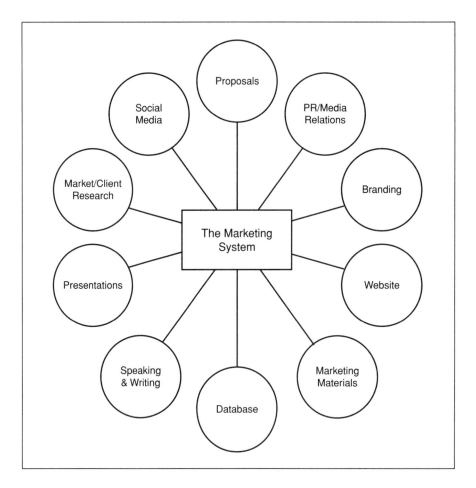

Figure 5.1   These 10 elements represent the core functions of any firm's marketing system. Success in firm positioning requires a planning process that integrates these ingredients with the firm's identity and market focus. (*Source:* SPARKS, The Center for Strategic Planning)

smaller pieces of the process will create an integrated structure that makes sense to all who utilize it.

Key Principles

When considering the development of the marketing system and its elements, the firm should include a number of key principles. The following six principles are offered as essentials for engaging in this development process at the firm level:

- It needs to be *philosophically based* on the firm's values and purpose. These will vary from firm to firm, so think about the higher order of values your firm is committed to. For instance, an idea firm is one that is always seeking a new edge or layer that will engage clients in seeing the project (and the firm) in a distinctive light. To the extent that sustainability is the more pervasive topic for the times, how might your firm present a unique set of thoughts and approaches that both reflects your values and offers something that other firms do not?

■ The next principle is to make the system *identity driven and market driven*. Once your firm has landed on the appropriate archetype and operating model, as discussed in Chapter 3, the leaders need to think hard about the implications for designing the marketing system that fits that choice. If your firm is a Community Leader, there are specific ways to proceed—to seek out new contacts, design a database, and put yourself in the best networks—that apply only to this archetype. Taking some time to understand these thoroughly and tailoring the system to fit their requirements will go a long way toward creating further integration. The same holds for markets. Although most firms work in a number of markets (perhaps five or six), typically fewer of these (maybe two or three) represent truly strategic opportunities. Distinguishing these from markets and projects that are less strategic to your ultimate plan will allow for a distinctive approach and investment that reflect those crucial choices.

■ A marketing system needs to be *positioning-motivated*. This means that it must look beyond individual project procurement, and seek to build the firm's story and brand in a compelling fashion. The use of a classic device such as a go/no-go decision making tool is a simple way of determining if the work fits the firm's direction, purpose, and desired position in the marketplace. Combine this thinking with the strategic/non-strategic aspect mentioned previously, and you'll be able to create the criteria for applying these decisions in a meaningful way.

■ The principles of *connectivity* and *interdependence* are vital when a firm is designing or redesigning a marketing system. Consider the 10 elements presented in Figure 5.1, and think about the connections each one has to other elements in the array. From a systems development perspective, these considerations should be taken in up-front, as opposed to later or never; they represent key opportunities to "see" where a well-developed system can go. An example of this is database development. A well-functioning database should provide all principals and staff with information and resources that are instantly accessible and useful. For many firms, the opposite is true.

Quite often, when the attempt is made to conduct some aspect of business that relies on a good database, the effort falls short of the potential payoff, frustrating many in the firm who understand how it really needs to function.

- Things change. Also, the essential things we need to accomplish using a good marketing system are often under intense time pressure. This leads us to the principle of *flexibility*, and the need to shift gears quickly without starting from scratch. The key to creating a flexible system is to construct it in a modular fashion. Similar to modular home design, and heavily influenced by software development standards for object-oriented system design, a flexible marketing system allows people to use the pieces they need or add an additional feature without starting over. When piecing together a newsletter for clients, staff should have ready access to the inventory of past articles written, conferences attended, and speeches given, as well as a myriad of other tidbits that are good for clients and prospects to know about. Having these subsets of data already in the marketing system makes it easy to construct a story around a theme that is ripe and ready to be told, without having to go to eight different people and beg them for scraps of information.

- The final principle for development of a marketing system is *accessibility*. While this has been hinted at in the preceding discussion, it's more a matter of the process of input and output. If any system is going to work, it needs to be enriched with a steady flow of information. In order to entice people to feed the machine, it must be designed so it's accessible on the input side. And technology is not always the factor at the first step of input, even though it's a strong consideration. Even handwritten input to a system can work, as long as steps two and three are set up and ready to turn those scribbles into something useful. The other end of the process, the output, also needs to be accessible so that occasional users of the modules can dive in, quickly find what they need, and move on.

For large firms, such a system is a necessity in order to meet the constant demands of a high-volume marketing effort. On the other end of the spectrum, a small firm might consider the implications of these efforts to be way over their head. In some ways, that's true, especially when it comes to software and development time. However, the principles and general approach for creating a marketing system should not waver. If a small firm has a series of hatboxes filled with information, organized and utilized as if it were a million-dollar system, they can have a successful marketing system.

For medium-sized firms, the choices can be a matter of timing: Where are we going, what do we need to get there, and when can we afford to invest in a more sophisticated approach to what is arguably the lifeblood of the firm?

Let's be clear: Developing a firm from the positioning standpoint involves much more than a few paragraphs in the latest proposal, a new website design, or a catchy tag line. Those are surface facets of positioning that may feel good for a few minutes, but don't penetrate markets in a powerful way. Positioning a design firm across all the aspects contained in this book should create power and influence for that firm, regardless of its size.

Now let's turn to a more in-depth exploration of the 10 elements of a marketing system.

The 10 Elements in Detail

As each of the 10 elements comes under consideration, the first crucial points to think about are: Where are we right now, and where do we want to be in the future? To assist in this exploration, three levels of achievement or competence are represented in Table 5-1. While there are many other ways to describe achievement (or current status) when reviewing these examples, these can provide a starting point to focus your firm's goals.

Proposals: Proposal development is one of the most essential marketing activities a firm undertakes. Given the time pressures that normally accompany proposal preparation, the first step is to be prepared at all times. This requires regular updating of all the key databases that are typically accessed for proposals. Examples of these databases include the following:

- Firm experience
- Resumes of key personnel
- Success stories and client references
- Proposal subtopic narratives
- Technical and business qualifications
- Project photography
- Layout templates and graphics
- Teaming profiles and experience of other professionals
- Staff registrations, accreditations, and professional achievements
- Project case studies
- Lists of articles, white papers, speaking engagements

TABLE 5-1: Marketing System Development

Elements	Basic Level	Intermediate Level	Advanced Level
Proposals	Answer the call	Team response	Develop a virtual experience
PR/Media Relations	Announcements, random/local	Planned/targeted, well-distributed stories	Firm thought leaders as sources for others
Branding	Tag line	Integrated identity	Branding your clients
Website	Electronic billboard	Content-rich, educational	Interactive communication tool
Marketing Materials	Brochures	Product development descriptions	Client solutions framework
Database	Individual lists	Firm-wide resource	Performance management & progress-tracking tool
Speaking & Writing	Describing firm project experience	Expose how we think and solve problems	Educate clients on their industry
Presentations	Discuss tasks, services, people	Present processes, decision-making criteria, team cohesion	Capture the right moments with passion and purpose
Market & Client Research	Casual, random research designed to generate leads, the next job	In-depth secondary research to determine significant trends and emerging client needs	Primary research to develop market education platform
Social Media	Borrow ideas from various sources	Systematic coverage and involvement	Generate followers and fans; be seen as a source

Of course, this is all typical grist for the proposal mill. What makes the difference when it comes to positioning? At the proposal stage, what makes the difference is setting up the next stage—specifically the presentation with which you plan to close the deal. For a new client, most firms want to provide a "to the letter" proposal response, in order to make an appropriate first impression. This usually means overloading the proposal with too much information, and presenting a fairly stiff and unimaginative response, to boot. Avoiding this mistake is mostly a matter of mindset, once you have your positioning traction in place. Firms that know who they are, for whom they wish to work, and what they can accomplish on projects need to present themselves with "controlled boldness." This approach conveys confidence that stops short of arrogance, and its purpose is to inform, but even more, to entice. How does a firm entice a client? It's done by exposing the thought processes and analytical skills of specific principals and staff. These nuggets need to be thought through, written, and placed in the proposal in a way that serves as an added level of assurance as the client is reading the response. This assurance not only adds depth to the proposal, it should also make the client want to meet with these intriguing professionals and make them part of the team. The same approach should apply to the individual who may have captured the lead that led to the proposal in the first place. Much of the time should be spent highlighting real people and how they think and solve problems. Every step of the marketing and positioning process needs to entice by showing what makes specific people on the staff interesting and capable, by convincing the client that these are the right people to work with. Do you ever feel that many sections of a proposal are dry, uninteresting, and mainly typical of what your firm and other firms are always saying? Have you ever thought of including photos of your people at work, in various sections of the proposal? Have you thought of sending the proposal accompanied by a small digital recording that can guide a client through the sections, recorded by a few of the key people who would be doing the work? Besides providing a guide, they can succinctly bring to life what certain experiences and accomplishments meant to them, and what excites them about this particular project.

These techniques and many more are all positioning tools that firms should be using to break through the clutter and sameness. Positioning is ultimately about people, passion, excitement, and a sense that the firm can create something great if it is given this specific opportunity. Be bold in positioning your proposals as storytelling tools that can come alive, and there's a likelihood great things will come your way.

Public Relations: Many design firms are deficient when it comes to effective public relations; however, there is evidence of a shift, as many firm websites now incorporate a more vibrant and updated "news" tab. Virtually every firm on the planet should be issuing at least one press release a month, and if you're not, find out what stories and news you're missing. If you aren't missing anything because it's not happening in the first place, set yourself a goal to make it happen. Good PR is an attractor. It's designed to tell a story, make an announcement, or acknowledge an accomplishment that the firm is proud of and wants to share. Effective PR means offering a window into the firm, highlighting people and key moments, and believing that others will in fact be interested in the information. Unfortunately, even those who engage in a decent amount of PR through press releases aren't too creative with the effort. Unless you're announcing the passing of a firm founder, consider every press release as an opportunity to make readers (clients and competitors, mostly) think differently about your firm.

One useful technique is the "dramatic and amazing headline" that comes before the actual story. Since your goal is to attract attention, instead of saying something bland, such as: FIRM ANNOUNCES APPOINTMENT OF THREE NEW PRINCIPALS, try a different approach: LOCAL FIRM SHAKES UP ORGANIZATION, NAMES NAMES. The story that follows can certainly be a fairly straightforward version of the announcement of new principals, but the idea is *to be noticed*.

The core purpose of public relations is to create interest in the firm, and make the people in the firm real and accessible. Instead of relying on official-sounding, arm's-length statements that could be ascribed to overly timid bureaucratic tendencies, make some of your releases more conversational in tone. Add a personal touch that gives the reader a surprise ending after the release has presented the requisite information on the particular topic. For example, here's the CEO being quoted at the conclusion of a standard announcement of a firm promotion: "And while we are all grateful to Michael for his many contributions to the firm's successes over the past 10 years, we know that what really matters most to him is our firm's annual fly-fishing outing. We expect another great performance from him this year, and look forward to his wonderful sense of humor as we novices try to master what he does with so little effort."

Don't be afraid to add humor and personal touches to these announcements every now and then. People will smile, you'll make them think, and the fly-fishing clients out there may just call up Michael to see where he's been catching some good fish.

On the positioning level, a press release should make the reader feel as if the firm is *leaning forward*, going somewhere important. This can be accomplished through the use of two techniques: (1) consistent messaging, and (2) pointing towards bigger things to come. The consistent messaging aspect is fairly direct, since the firm will have established its identity, purpose, operating model, branding focus, and role in the design world. Some of those words, phrases, sentences, tag lines, and highlights need to appear unfailingly in any official communication the firm puts out. When your messages are clear and consistent, it trains readers to believe that *you believe* what you're saying. Regarding bigger things to come, let's say the press release is related to a new project award. Besides describing all the normal aspects of the client, facility type, location, construction value, LEED intentions, and so forth, be sure to include a statement about how this project will make good use of your firm's skills in an area such as sustainability. Then make sure you have an extended comment about that key topic, for instance: "We're excited about undertaking this project because it represents an excellent model for the marriage of preservation and

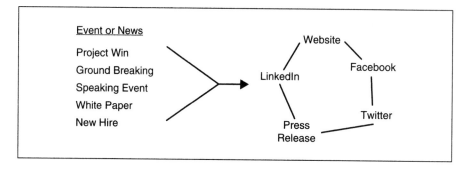

Figure 5.2 In order to maximize firm exposure and recognition, new tools must be added at all times. This chart shows how social media outlets can enhance networking and public relations efforts. (*Source:* SPARKS, The Center for Strategic Planning)

sustainability to create a unified concept for such a vital structure in this city. This particular experience for our firm will allow us to make a significant contribution to the research efforts we're engaged in with Big University regarding climate change." This statement sends a very strong message to the reader, and every firm needs to find, shape, and utilize its *leaning forward* ideas and bring them to life in its PR efforts.

Although social media will be discussed later in this chapter, there is a strong correlation with the PR-driven positioning of a firm that is characterized by the social media ring, depicted in Figure 5.2.

This approach to systemic connectivity when it comes to public relations helps ensure that the firm isn't relying purely on the traditional outlets for the dissemination of significant news and events. This approach also allows non-marketing staff to participate in the process, which can function as a low-overhead methodology to support the firm's positioning goals.

Branding

Brand creation can seem to be a somewhat mystifying concept at times, and for professional services firms, it can appear to be a fruitless endeavor. Yet what is true and will remain true is that if you are able to create brand recognition within the minds of your target audience, it will be your most valuable asset by far. Your brand is the essence of your positioning, the distilled version of the meaning and purpose that you need to have in order to capture client mindshare among your many competitors. However, keep in mind that brand development does not require a signature phrase or catchy tag line. When done most effectively, branding will begin and end with your firm's name. When this level of recognition and respect has been achieved, the firm can then establish brand extensions. HOK Sport is the classic illustration in terms of design firms. And now that the firm is called Populous, the challenge for them isn't necessarily to make Populous as recognizable as HOK Sport was. It's more a matter of making sure people make the connection: "It's the same firm it always was." With that connection in place, virtually no brand value will be lost.

Gensler is another strong example of branding through their name. They are synonymous with corporate and workplace design throughout the world. They may utilize other tag lines or descriptors at times, but those elements aren't where the value lies. The marketing chief at Gensler can wake up tomorrow and add or remove a tag line or phrase from the website or the next printing of materials, and the downside risk is zero from a branding perspective. Reliance on a tag line is one of the first pitfalls in branding, from a professional services angle. Branding doesn't need to include the creation of the most captivating tag line ever written. While that aspect can be a valuable addition, it shouldn't become an all-consuming focus. Simply put, successful branding begins with an unrelenting focus on one element: a market, a project type, a service, a point of view, a particular design sensibility, an approach—something that serves as the internally recognized center of the universe for the firm. With that established, the synergies that lead to various branding opportunities and choices are in place. Working backwards through a tag line is a difficult way to make a brand.

Other brand development methods can be found through brand extension or through the branding of specific services. Certainly, the HOK Sport case was in essence a brand extension, but interestingly, the extension took on a more powerful presence than the HOK name alone. Much of this development had to do with the fact that their projects of choice became icons in many of the world's largest cities, catering to the interests of many millions of people, not to mention all the television exposure. This halo effect doesn't happen with the market for libraries or senior housing.

Although the vast majority of design firms haven't spent a lot of time concerned about their "brand," this will continue to change over the coming years. Why? The answer is that a stronger identity is required in order to be noticed, beyond being an architect or engineer with experience. The final stages of commoditization of professional services are occurring in the current reset of the U.S. economy, and most firms are struggling just to stay afloat and maintain their essential livelihoods—never mind branding or re-branding themselves. Yet that is exactly what they should be doing. The more aggressive and resourceful firms are taking this opportunity to reposition themselves for the next round of opportunities. While many are jumping on the clean energy/sustainability/green bandwagon, some are building their own proprietary bandwagons. This is the better way to go, and their branding essence will reflect their individuality as their position strengthens. A strong brand develops from the inside out, and expresses a greater purpose or capability than the current set of projects on the boards.

Consider the ocean separating the following two branding phrases, when it comes to conveying meaning. "Serving the Entire Midwest" might be an accurate statement, but is it compelling? "Creating Progressive Educational Environments" is a much better version for a firm wishing to connect with institutions that are themselves on the leading edge. Such institutions will immediately be compelled to learn more about your firm if you clearly express that as your purpose. With the first slogan, you simply imply a willingness to drive from state to state. The second declares your thought leadership in a key field, which of course, you need to back up with depth and the evidence of your efforts. Consider the effect of a strong brand on recruiting top talent. Good talent will always check you out from a distance to see if there are signs of compatibility. If all they see on your website is a listing of services and a few standard project photos and descriptions, they will likely move on.

With so many firms working in a number of diverse markets, creating a brand image with a true market focus can be difficult. The natural tendency, therefore, is to skip the whole branding idea entirely, or to opt for a client-service-oriented image. While there's nothing wrong with excellence in client service, is that truly the image you're striving for? Frankly, any client worth their salt now expects top-drawer client service and support from a firm, so making it your headline is similar to hanging the sign "Air Conditioned" near the entrance to a modern restaurant. Better ideas come from asking yourself: What are your insights into the future of communities? Or housing? Or civic gathering places such as museums and theaters? How can you express these thoughts in a succinct fashion and draw in the mindshare of those reading your materials or visiting your website?

For many firms, tackling these questions in order to create a lasting brand means making some tough decisions about market focus, investing in talent and research, and having the patience to believe in the power of an idea. A defensive approach to branding isn't a viable route to success and recognition, and given the possible increases in competition over the coming decade, it won't be enough to save a firm that doesn't truly believe in itself.

How a firm discovers its brand and manages the permeation of that identity into every aspect of the firm is a unique story for each firm. The following case is one example of how a firm can shape and influence the process.

CASE STUDY: COOPER CARRY, ATLANTA, GEORGIA

BRANDING AND THE ART OF MARKETING

Dig into the archives of Cooper Carry's marketing ideas, writings, and materials, and you're likely to find more than one item that makes you pause and ponder the marketing mindset that created these pieces. Perhaps it will be the intriguing, colorful, and fairly chaotic poster called "The Discovery Process," an original design created for the firm's science and technology studio. Or, it might be one of the issues of *Here*, the Cooper Carry magazine that combines high-level graphics, ideas, art, and whimsy with plenty of statistics and snippets of world news and cultural movements, to whet your appetite for more. Possibly, you'll take a look at the Middle English account of the Battle of Scholastica, and want to dive into the Internet to learn more about that battle in 1355 between "Towne and Gowne." Then, if you're lucky enough to get your hands on a 125-page spiral-bound book with the title *Vision, Strategies, Brand for the Third Generation* (*VSB*), the mystery of the marketing mindset will begin to solve itself. A blending of historical perspective on the firm with project highlights and a keen sense of direction for the future, *VSB* outlines an informed view on the possibilities of marketing and positioning strategies.

Clearly, the firm has developed a passion for marketing that drives it forward. Since the early '90s, this marketing vision has shaped Cooper Carry into an innovative and substantial firm with 280 staff spread among offices in Atlanta; Washington, DC; Alexandria, Virginia; and Newport Beach, California. *VSB* represents a call to arms for greater differentiation in the sea of design firms. Pope Bullock, executive vice president at Cooper Carry, says that 2005 was a real turning point in the firm's view of what needed to be done. "After researching the problem for quite a while, we knew we needed to differentiate ourselves from our competitors by using resources typically untapped by our profession. Successful firms have compelling differentiation stories. We needed to learn from product marketers who understand the process better than service marketers do," Bullock recalls.

One of the first problems to tackle was a lack of clarity and consistency regarding the firm's identity. The continual addition of new principals meant that new ideas about a collective identity were essential, if the firm was to overcome the common industry hurdle of practice groups that were out of alignment with the firm as a whole. The firm saw a major challenge and opportunity to develop broader capabilities for marketing throughout the firm, moving from the traditional view of marketing purely as a business function to the view of marketing as a philosophy. The tougher question became "How?" and, in 2005, firm leaders designed an answer. Figure 5.3 shows the elements of the road map Cooper Carry used to guide the overall process.

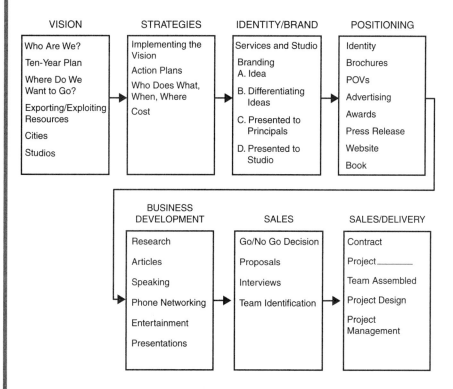

Figure 5.3   The marketing process developed by Cooper Carry helps ensure that the message and positioning aspects are consistent with their long-term vision and purpose. (*Source:* Cooper Carry)

As *VSB* continues, it moves away from the big picture proposition about marketing, to cover the history of the firm, along with selected projects and a brief graphical recap of some of the firm's marketing materials throughout the decades. "We were stuck," says Bullock. "And we lacked the fundamental brand standards I felt were needed to steer the firm in a more compelling direction." That direction began with a series of meetings about differentiation and branding, but since there were no recipes available for implementation, it became a matter of trial and error. Cooper Carry began the creation of an asymmetrical identity for each practice group, purposely allowing the overall firm identity to reside more in the shadows. Each team refined their marketing message, and began designing the specific approaches and techniques for getting the message out to clients. Principals at the firm felt that keeping the firm's identity subdued, while practice leaders took to the fore, was the real key to reaching for the most creative messages. "Many larger firms refuse to move beyond the broad message of the mothership," Bullock notes. "This can overwhelm the discussion and the practice leader isn't getting the focus needed to carve out a more unique point of view. The result is you maintain the hierarchical structure, and all expectations flow all the way to the top."

This creation of a sub-branding marketing culture also creates a new class of thought leaders who become known as much individually as the firm is known. The process is also well suited for re-creation and exportation to new offices and principals, since it puts them in a more responsible role for marketing than simply landing the next project. Additionally, this model added a depth of market focus and expertise that went beyond the facility that was being designed. Cooper Carry wanted their practice and brand leaders to be choreographers for the retail or hospitality or university campus experience that the end users would participate in. And once they took the concept that far, it was logical to extend their services into branding work for client identity enhancement as well. This entire package of ideas led to the Cooper Carry identity tag line called The Center for Connective Architecture.

Another element of the market positioning strategy the firm developed was to accentuate ideas over experience. While experience across the firm is certainly valuable, they no longer saw it as a powerful source of differentiation. They succeeded in creating a brand identity for the Mainstreet studio with only one project under their belt. The quality of the ideas the firm focused on made the difference, and the creation of this edge opened new doors fairly quickly.

This approach to marketing worked well for the firm, but what of the effects of the downturn and continuing recession? According to

Bullock, Cooper Carry is sticking with their model and marketing philosophy, even as certain markets shrink and shift in terms of their needs. "We saw the writing on the wall early enough in 2009 to make a few important shifts in our focus. We quickly established three federal practice groups to pursue the opportunities that were there, and yet we'll still be ready when opportunities bubble up in the markets we were previously engaged with. While the federal system certainly has a unique set of rules to abide by, we're finding our essential approach to marketing still works. Once you engrain the ideas of market focus and branding in your thinking, you begin to understand it has value regardless of the nature of the client entity."

And as in most firms, some of the larger marketing expenditures have been trimmed, as markets and budgets get adjusted to the new reality. What may have been a "wow" marketing piece for the hospitality market has now become electronic content for something like transit-oriented development. While acknowledging that some of these market changes have been substantial, the firm's leaders are committed to continuing the flow of creativity that comes from the marketing philosophy they have nurtured over the past decade.

Bullock concludes: "Where we apply ourselves is always subject to change with the ups and downs of markets and economies. Our focus is on how we think creatively about each individual market, regardless of public or private, boom or bust. These concepts will help us both thrive and survive, and we're looking forward to finding out how we can use them in ways we haven't even thought of yet."

Website

Successfully branding a firm requires an integrated approach that considers all of the various technologies and physical resources available. Over the past 15 years, the website has come to function as the hub of a firm's essential message to the world. However, take a look around at design industry sites—most of them are lacking in effort, functionality, and purpose. Today's websites should function like the daily newspaper. They need to be current, varied, and accurate. Most firms consider the website "fresh" if it was redesigned two years ago, and this just isn't the case. Many sites lack recent news, press releases, exciting project or organizational updates, and blogs. As one example of a firm that has tackled these issues, take a look at vmdo.com. VMDO Architects is a Charlottesville, Virginia–based firm specializing in K–12 and higher education. Spend some time on their website, and you'll find a steady feed of news and information about their projects and clients, in addition to all the other requisite website trappings. The site is attractive, informative, and fresh, giving it a feel that speaks to VMDO's certainty about their positioning and purpose as a firm.

Design firms seeking to enhance their Web presence need to think through their options. A vibrant website is a commitment, but it needn't be an expensive chore. For some firms, the best choice is to work with a marketing and communications firm that can assist with branding, messaging, materials, website, and other critical communications needs. Although these services can be expensive, the cost will only deter you if it exceeds your commitment to the overall positioning process. Firms that simply cannot afford that type of outside help should consider a service such as Canright, a website design and software development company in Oregon that specializes in sites for architects. With reasonable pricing and flexible plans, such services can be the right choice for many firms with limited budgets. One pitfall connected with website development is being sold on SEO (search engine optimization), which is a decent tool, but can be accomplished at the level needed by most design firms as a simple in-house exercise. Spending tens of thousands of dollars on SEO is foolish for most design firms.

As with many facets of the marketing system, firm leaders need to be viewing the situation through the lens of competitive positioning, as opposed to the lens of merely updating a tool to look better. A website needs to be *felt* by the potential clients who arrive there. It should hold their interest for a good while, and make them want to return to see what else they can learn. This is attraction, this is pull, and this is how firms need to create a more efficient and effective marketing system if they are to compete successfully in the future.

Marketing Materials

When firms aren't promoting their people and their ideas as the main reasons for clients to conduct business with them, it's possible they will over-produce and over-complicate their pile of marketing materials. Aside from the time and expense factors involved with a mountain of materials, words and pictures are a poor substitute for passion, enthusiasm, and professional pride. Yet, every firm needs a collection of materials for their mailings, conference visits, seminars, and other events where there's a chance to introduce the firm to new prospects. From a positioning standpoint, clarity and simplicity work best. The more you feel compelled to produce pages and pages of materials, especially related to basic services and project experience, the more you need to turn around and head in the other direction. The exception to this is when a firm has developed a research-based piece that requires or deserves the in-depth attention of the reader. However, a piece like that isn't typically mailed out to many thousands of clients. It typically will be provided to a client or prospect after some initial interest has been established, either through the website or a direct mail piece that triggers a mailing.

If you return to the concepts around firm identity and purpose, most marketing materials can work in a page or two, using one or a few of those aspects connected to a person in the firm, a client, or an idea. Obviously, any branding identity the firm has developed is also a fertile source for connectivity to a more expanded message. As shown in the case study of Cooper Carry, the firm has done an excellent job at two ends of the marketing materials spectrum. Their *Here* magazine, rich in production values and visual value, exemplifies a firm's desire to expose their soul and essence through their materials. Colorful, complex, and edgy, the magazine is the type that makes you want to be sure you receive the next year's issue, just to immerse yourself in thoughtful reaction. Their other versions of marketing materials, in addition to the poster already referenced, were typically simple pieces that acted more like a greeting card than a marketing tool. With the endless possibilities of what can be placed on a website, the era of "big materials" is likely shrinking. If you're designing something to send out to folks in the physical realm, it should be based on your identity/purpose commitment or your brand, and should highlight either a person or a *leaning forward* idea that the firm is engaged with. Anything else really isn't worth the time and cost to develop, print, and distribute.

In addition to pointing clients to your website for fully developed marketing stories, project histories, and the like, another approach is to go electronic in the other direction. With the crunch of the recession slashing marketing budgets, many firms are creating unique and powerful materials to send over email. Obviously, this increases the pressure on database creation and maintenance, and should be as good an excuse as any to get that problem addressed once and for all. One particular opportunity to think about, once you have a client's permission to send them materials online, is surveys and other interactive media. Many firms use SurveyMonkey or a similar service to conduct client and market research, and once a client feels comfortable with these electronic exchanges, you may be able to "touch" them a few times a year and gain some valuable insights. In this sense, even client satisfaction research qualifies as a piece of marketing material, especially if the firm embeds the message of "who they are" in and around the questions. The best rules to keep in mind when it comes to marketing materials are summarized as follows:

- Entice as much as you inform.
- Ideas are more important than experience.
- People with ideas need to move to the forefront.
- Create pieces that point clients to act or access another firm resource.
- Be aggressive in migrating from physical to electronic wherever possible.

The Big Shift will mean new ways of connecting, informing, and deciding. Firms should be experimenting with all types of media and approaches as this shift continues to undo the traditions of the past two decades or so. And in terms of bringing the core to the edge, the best starting point may be wiping the entire table (and cabinets) clean and taking out a new sheet of paper to reenvision the entire environment genre, and how your firm should fit into that picture.

Database

The firm database of contacts, connections, clients, and organizations is undoubtedly the most neglected marketing resource with the most potential for payoff. That's not to say some larger firms don't have their act together in this regard—many do. But for small and medium-sized firms, it's often a nightmare of a project that gets brought up every 12 months and is never, ever resolved satisfactorily. At the half-competent level is another set of firms where individual principals and project managers may have a decent collection of complete electronic records, but the missing link is building that distributed collection into a viable firm-wide resource. From a diagnostic perspective, a firm unwilling to create a complete database of contacts, given all of the potential uses and inherent value contained in it, is unlikely to be deeply concerned about their position in the marketplace. From a humorous perspective, the good news will be that when they've gone out of business, there will be no one to tell!

Clearly, the most valuable use of a database is in relation to business development. The secondary value is in supporting client service initiatives. In both cases, the information should be seen as a representation of the networks that are functioning both outside the firm's immediate purview, and within it. The database is the people we know and need to keep track of, combined with those we want to know and get our word out to.

The best approach for keeping the already-known contacts up to date is to send an inexpensive mailing once or twice a year that includes a return, in case the individual has moved on. This can be displaced by electronic confirmations, if desired, but keep in mind that some physical, thought-provoking snail mail is still a good idea once in a while. On the business development side of things, the single best way to build or update a list of potential clients is to conduct primary research. Wrapping the database project within this initiative not only ensures that it gets done, it also provides substantial added value. Once a firm knows the positioning ingredients that will make up its ultimate success, it needs to generate the list of institutions and companies that represent that target. With that list in hand, it's recommended that the firm consult a professional in market research, who can (1) obtain the best available individual contact information, and (2) conduct a market research study on the firm's behalf. This investment deepens the firm's commitment to its target audience, helps solve the database problem, and forces the issue of taking a meaningful stand on positioning in the marketplace. In fact, the more certain a firm is about its positioning, the better the survey will be received. It's quite imaginable that many owners get bombarded with the same tiring line of questions about "what they're looking for in a design firm." Those approaches are actually quite transparent; it's clear that the firm is fishing for a lead, as opposed to qualifying the potential client with regard to the firm's higher purpose. There is power in certainty of purpose, and more firms need to develop that tool, to sift through the long list of potential clients and find those who will truly appreciate their skills and passion.

In closing on the database issue, there is no particular magic about how to do it; most firms already know about programs and services like ACT!, Constant Contact, and VerticalResponse. But as with the entire issue of positioning—of moving the firm beyond a set of projects and into the place in the market where preparation and opportunity collide—it's really a matter of willingness to do the dirty work that resides in the details. Turn those details into an integral part of the marketing system, and then you can move your thinking forward to the next step—how you can turn the database into new projects that affirm what the firm has chosen to accomplish.

Speaking and Writing

Speaking for Professional Success

When it comes to establishing professional status as a thought leader in the design industry, the activities of speaking and writing are at the top of the list. These, along with the production of original research, form a powerful triumvirate that gets individuals and firms noticed and sought after. However, beyond the basics of simply engaging in these activities, there are certain ways to perform them that can make a tremendous difference in the outcomes achieved.

Speaking can be pursued in various ways, such as: at a seminar hosted by the firm under its own control, typically with an audience of clients or prospects; at a professional association event, such as the AIA; or at an industry event where the audience is your target market. Each of these venues carries its own generalized purpose. The seminar may be seen as a way to further cement or extend existing relationships, while the professional conference is usually used to showcase the firm's progress, and perhaps look for new partner relationships. The client industry event is clearly a matter of networking for leads for new work, while displaying the firm's commitment to that audience over the longer term.

Looking at the in-house seminar first, it carries with it a few pros and cons. It's a good way to get your feet wet if you're new to public speaking, or if the material is new and unfamiliar. It's considered a safer crowd, more or less, although the size of the group can make for an awkward moment or two if tough questions come up—especially regarding specific project work recently completed or currently under way. From a speaking perspective, everyone needs practice, and a few in-house seminars a year are a great way to do research, get feedback, and work out kinks in a developing presentation or topic area. Care should be taken not to over-speak in these situations, however. More than two presentations in one four-hour session can push the audience into the glazed-eyes zone. On the other hand, having too little to say in a formal address can leave the room under-stimulated. When looking to present primarily to test out ideas or conduct small-group research, be sure to set the tone accordingly. Most presenting is done with the mindset of "I've got to come across as the expert," which can be overplayed in the smaller setting. The best approach is to develop a few modules of material meant to stimulate questions and discussion, and intersperse them with audience participation. While you may begin the presentation in a stand-up, fairly formal mode, wind that down fairly quickly, after no more than 15 minutes have elapsed. Conduct the second module while seated, and perhaps a third module using a handout instead of the projection screen. Once you've laid out your thoughts and premises for each module, shift to the learning mode, and have the clients teach while you take notes. This shift of power and responsibility, even for a short while, goes a long way toward keeping the session balanced and energized. Be sure to set up very specific follow-up steps for more in-depth discussions, collection of additional data, or the forwarding of a meeting summary.

From a positioning point of view, make sure your *leaning forward* ideas are out there, and tell the audience what else you may be looking for in the future, to further develop your thinking. Ask for additional contacts from them, to develop new sources, partners, research opportunities, or most certainly new clients. Brainstorm a future event, perhaps 6–12 months down the road, that includes a broader, larger audience, and gain their views on the viability and structure of such an event. Lastly, food also works wonders for getting people to relax and open up, so make sure the snacks and caffeine flow freely throughout the meeting.

Speaking at a professional association event can be seen as a big step in the professional development of an architect or engineer. Taking the stage in front of peers for the first time is a bit like being Crosby, Stills & Nash at Woodstock. All of music's biggest stars were watching to see how they would do, and they had only played together twice previously. Yet, things seemed to turn out just fine for them, so with that dollop of inspiration, forge ahead.

The first choice to make when seeking to present at a large regional or national professional conference deals with the big picture: Will this talk be about a specific project? Will it be about a big idea? Or will it be about a process or technical issue that sits a bit more behind the scenes? Each of these choices requires a unique approach to speaking, and in the preparation of the materials. Most speakers will use the big screen for these presentations, plus at least a few handouts, often required by the hosting organization. The typical problem with a talk about a specific project is that it becomes as dry as burnt toast within about 15 minutes. What's often presented is a litany of features, measurements, tools, requirements, and all the myriad activities connected to the tasks of design. A better approach is to talk about the people involved first, then make the required points about the technical matters. Of course, when writing up the plan for the presentation, the speaker should be clear about how the discussion will unfold, so as not to disappoint those who are looking only for a list-driven technical presentation. The fact is, 80 percent of those presentations could be conveyed in writing just as well, and then we wouldn't see a few dozen attendees (along with the speaker) crawling out the door after 90 minutes of virtual torture.

In these instances, the speaker needs to make a strong attempt to engage the audience in not only the technical aspects, but also the "how" of dealing with clients or other service partners on these issues. Include a human interest story (with a focus on your amazing problem-solving skills) every 15 minutes, to display your deeper perceptions about the entire process, and to extract a few stories along the same line from the audience. Keep five or six handwritten cheat sheets in front of you, with potential stories you can use, and jump on them when the timing is right. Although judgment by peers may feel a bit frightening at times, the good news about these events is that you can reflect openly on the professional challenges involved in doing your work. This kind of sharing can strengthen the connection with the audience, enrich the discussion, and perhaps even lead to new insights or breakthroughs about how to manage clients through an issue or obstacle.

The third venue, the client-market conference, is generally considered to be at the top of the food chain for professionals who speak and present. And for good reason, because the expectation is to attract new clients, but a few missteps can sink your ship fairly quickly. First, keep in mind that these are people who will enjoy real-life stories mixed in with their information cocktail. In these environments, it's best to think of yourself as an orchestrator, one who is licensed to take the audience where it needs to go, as opposed to where you planned for it to go. This doesn't mean you don't cover your carefully prepared material—of course you do. But how you do it, your pace, and the emotion you generate will make the difference between an impressive effort and one that's forgettable. Right from the start in these situations, it's best to be deferential, casual, and somewhat humorous. One easy technique to kick things off is to scan that day's newspaper for a story or event that can be connected to some aspect of your talk or their industry, or provide some other common perspective. Some self-deprecating comments having to do with your travels to the destination, the night in the hotel, or another type of shared experience work fine as well. Most folks are so nervous or anxious that they almost immediately jump into the first slide, and the opportunity to connect is lost. If you take that approach, your material had better be very, very good or very short, because you have now inadvertently set yourself up as the person whose material compels admiration. Most of us simply can't risk that.

The body of material at an industry presentation ought to be about the audience, the ones you want to turn into your new clients. If it's about you, your firm, architecture, or even an idea that relates to design, you run the risk of being interesting while not connecting. A large percentage of this type of speaking engagement must be *about them*, with you presenting your version of *their view of the world*. This allows you to seek agreement and assent, which makes an audience feel good. It also provides plenty of opportunity to veer off the prepared material and display the kinds of skills you want them to buy from you, meaning empathy, appreciation, passion, communication, and thoughtfulness.

A technique to use to prepare in advance for this aspect of a presentation is to look at each slide individually, and determine if it should be graded a U, a T, or a W. The U means it's mostly about Us (or me, the presenter), and those need to be minimized. T means it's about Them, a good thing, and these should represent at least 50 percent of what you're presenting. W means it's a We slide, which is a recommended sentiment to have running through the final third of the presentation. Look at this balance carefully to get a sense of how the information will be received. Consider technical information to be a U in most cases, unless its source is the industry you're presenting to.

Writing for Professional Recognition

Speaking may be taken as a challenge to get through the next 90 minutes, but writing can be seen as its evil twin, often requiring greater time and effort to produce something noteworthy. Almost every firm has at least one principal who has been published, or intends to move up the ladder of professional achievement by developing writing skill. Three basic formats exist for this endeavor: articles, white papers, and books. A fourth, the firm's blog, is emerging as an additional outlet for professional writing.

Writing an article for the typical design industry magazine or website is a good way to begin getting your sea legs. From a positioning perspective, be sure to choose a topic or idea that plays into the firm's vision and dovetails with an interest that you are willing to build on over time. While simple project profile articles are acceptable as a starting point, they may not convey a big enough message about your firm, which should be your ultimate goal. The easiest way to make this distinction is to think "descriptive" versus "exploratory." Descriptive articles are a dime a dozen; the exposure is fine, but they aren't often great attractors to the firm. Exploratory articles, which can certainly weave in specifics of projects, carry a greater message about your view of the world, and will provide a stronger platform for generating substantive response from interested readers. As with speaking, the balance of U, T, and W should be considered in preparing an outline. One way to achieve that perspective is to think about the road map you'd like to draw for your next client's experience with your firm. If you write from that point of view, most of what you say about your firm or your experience can be combined with descriptions of how it will benefit the readers if they work with you. Also, be sure to include the *leaning forward* aspects, best used at the beginning and ending of an article, to represent the rest of the story as a steppingstone to the future, not necessarily the height of your achievements.

A white paper offers a few distinct advantages and challenges for a professional services writer. The advantages are that you have a clean slate upon which to explore ideas, possibilities, opinions, and prognostications without the tether of a particular project or other current limitations. A white paper is a great starting point for a principal at a firm to make a statement that expresses the firm's positioning plan, and can therefore be seen as an inspirational piece as much as an attempt to develop new business. White papers are also very useful for making thought partner connections that go beyond a particular project. They can be distributed in private to selected contacts in academia, professional services, and trusted client environments, and serve as an anchor for future discussions about "What if?" or "How can we get there?" Even those principals who aren't thinking about writing a white paper should set up a Google search alert or some similar device to keep abreast of new, in-depth thinking that hits the Internet. Many professionals regularly flip through the requisite collection of periodicals, but too few are actively seeking out the best thought leaders and writings that can help shift perspective and long term goals.

Compared to the other choices, writing a book can be seen as a huge undertaking, perhaps best left for retirement. And it is a large commitment that not many have the time and inclination for, even considering the relatively high prestige that comes with publishing. Monographs can be expensive and time-consuming projects, with somewhat questionable business development value for the typical firm. For most firms, however, an alternative path that still winds up in book form should be considered. Self-publishing a series of essays around a topic or two can be accomplished as a group effort, especially if one principal has the skills and interest to guide the process. Consider something as basic as *Essays on Views of Sustainability for the Hospitality Industry*. There are already a good number of starting points available through existing publications, blogs, white papers, and so forth. Shifting your role to half editor, half writer, you already have a running start on your topic, and probably a good number of other writers or sources who might be willing to let you use their ideas or previous publications in your book. From a marketing perspective, this approach displays commitment, ascension of the ladder of reputation, and a willingness to open up broad areas of discussion with your clients, as opposed to simply marketing for the next project. Self-publishing such a product is inexpensive enough to allow you to print a few thousand copies for free distribution at speaking engagements, as well as for targeted mailings. A publication of this style needn't be voluminous; even 120 pages of good material with a great cover and upgraded paper stock can make a lasting impression.

Although the topic of social media is covered separately in this chapter, the subject of blogs deserves mention here. A firm blog is a good idea for a lot of reasons, but simply as a method for practicing the thought-formation and writing process, it can be the right vehicle for getting started. The blog called Life at Hok is an excellent example of how this tool is developing, and many firms are quickly moving towards a similar space as this Big Shift continues to unfold around us.

For both speaking and writing activities, an annual plan should be devised as part of the positioning development effort. Some firms may even establish criteria akin to those for gaining tenure at a university, whereby aspiring and current principals are required to publish and speak a certain number of times per year. The fact is that both speaking and writing at a certain level of proficiency are required in order for a firm to be viewed as an expert-level leader in its field of focus. The rewards of these significant efforts will continue to accrue to those firms that are willing to make the complete investment in the positioning process.

Client Presentations

Client presentations designed to win new work represent several of the most critical and nerve-racking realities of living and dying by the project. For many firms, these relatively brief exercises offer a clear window into their strengths and shortcomings, and can serve as either a joyful affirmation or a dose of discouraging reality. When the presenting team is scrambling to figure out the best way to showcase their skills as a function of their investment in their position in the marketplace, confidence runs high, and the focus is mostly on the known weaknesses and shortcomings of their competitors. This knowledge drives the placement of key points to deliver and discussions to engage the client in, so your firm is seen to outshine others on the short list. Oral presentations, combined with the materials designed to back up the presenters, are mostly about credibility and chemistry. This events test a team's ability to read people well, and to respond deftly to the subtle and overt cues from their small audience. Janet Sanders, PhD, FSMPS, has written an excellent article on the topic, available in the third edition of the SMPS and BNi Building News *Marketing Handbook for the Design and Construction Professional*, recommended reading for all who are seeking to sharpen their skills in this area.

The harsh reality of our new era is that competition will continue to increase, and the hit rates of many firms will continue to drop as hungry and talented firms expand their targets, and clients seek out the best value along with the right level of risk. From a positioning standpoint, it could be said that a firm is correctly positioned if it continues to get short-listed on the projects it expects to win, and so the positioning considerations are minimal for the presentation itself. Another view is that many firms make the short-list cut as a result of historical or traditional connections with the client or industry, or through regional familiarity, but that their hit rates don't reflect an upward trajectory. Is there anything that positioning can do, given those conditions? The answer may lie more in trying to ascertain the client's patterns than in positioning per se. Assuming your firm has done all the right things relative to developing your place in the market, why wouldn't you win twice as many jobs as before? It may well be because clients are undergoing a change in thinking themselves, and sometimes a few of the firms on the short list are there more for old time's sake than for real consideration. Look carefully at a client's short-listing patterns before you develop a proposal for what seems to be a well-matched project. Talk to a friendly competitor or two who didn't make the cut with that same client recently, even after getting short-listed. Consider conducting a survey of representative clients to try to determine shifts in industry thinking about facility projects, and certainly read more from market publications with an eye towards emerging hot buttons that might be the make-or-break difference in final selection.

The fact is, virtually every firm that makes it onto a short list is qualified to do the job. Additionally, many client panels know whom they prefer before they sit down to listen to the presentations. The positioning puzzle for a successful design firm therefore remains a matter of wisely choosing your targets, your focus, and your long-term commitments. Any firm that begins losing 60–80 percent after being short-listed needs to take serious stock of how its self-perception aligns with client patterns and larger market shifts. Very much like an earthquake with aftershocks, the Big Shift will continue to surprise even the most talented and typically well-prepared leaders and firms.

Social Media

Comments on a Generation of Marketing Evolution

When Sandra March talks about the changes that have occurred in the marketing of architectural services over the past 20 years, her voice suddenly fills with amazement. "Do you know what really astounds me most about what's happening right now?" she asks. "I get new followers on Twitter almost every day!" According to March, the viral aspects of current technologies make things much more exciting than they were when she started out as Ashley McGraw's first marketing director. Now she's in the position of chief marketing officer, and those 20 years seem like a blur. Stopping to consider the changes, she rattles off a few that seem somewhat quaint or almost surreal. There weren't many trade shows for the firm to attend in their Central New York market, and the ones that came along were undeniably low key and low budget. Tabletop displays with a few brochures or other handouts were the common fare, with no expensive graphics or presentations to point to. Email was still in the future in 1990, and websites weren't yet on the radar screen.

Fast-forward another 10 years to 2000. Sandra seems to feel that was the beginning of the modern era. "We put up our first billboard-style website in the late '90s, and moved into more powerful graphics and presentation software. The economy was strong in our markets, and we began to experience several exhilarating growth phases. Green building and sustainability began to develop, and there was a clear sense that competition was increasing quickly. Our biggest problem was in hiring talent—it seemed no architects were available for many of those years." Of course, that condition completely reversed itself in a matter of a few years, as the boom created a large number of overworked architects, followed fairly quickly by a flood of resumes into the firm, as 2008 turned against the industry. "We've been very fortunate to have sailed through the current recession with another record year in 2009. But now as a function of less work available to all firms, we clearly see the level of competition rising again," said March.

From a marketing perspective, March sees her greatest challenge as working to keep client service and satisfaction levels as high as possible. "When economies and markets slow down, design firms ultimately have to trim staff in order to make it through. Those cuts put pressure on everyone to balance their workload with responding to and anticipating client needs, and that's something we work very hard at doing well."

So which aspects of the next 10 years does Sandra anticipate the most? "We've hired our first in-house engineer, and that will give us a few new opportunities to expand and re-position our services, which is great. We've undertaken a re-branding project for the firm that shows a lot of promise, and I'm anticipating a new interactive website including a blog for the firm's thought leaders and the entire staff to contribute to. And finally, this social media explosion has me very enthused. The new network connections we're making every week—every day—are really contributing to the knowledge sources of the firm, something I wasn't too convinced of before now. But seeing it happen, and participating myself on a regular basis, I'm completely convinced we need to be on that train and not look back."

Generational Shifts Take Hold

Even though the design industry typically lags when it comes to embracing new methods and technologies for marketing, the rapid rise of social media penetrates the industry deeper every day. And even though a company blog can be considered half social media tool and half website feature, it serves as a good example of the nature of the generational shift that's under way. Life at HOK is the blog for the St. Louis–headquartered firm HOK, and is a prime illustration of how to approach the blogging arena. Located on the Web at hoklife.com, it was started in 2008 and has received considerable attention from the industry and the media since its debut. With postings that range from grieving the loss of two more industry magazines to ideas on mastering Revit, the blog functions as a source of information about the industry in general, as well as specifics about HOK's endeavors. The blog isn't censored, and that authenticity is a strategic aspect of HOK's positioning plan when it comes to recruiting. With dozens of bloggers making contributions from around the world, the firm sees the blog as a way to keep the firm on the cutting edge. Add to that the networking aspects, and it's rapidly becoming a formidable force in the firm's reach. Consider the following listing of HOK's network presence, which starts with their website:

HOK.com **http://hok.com/**

HOK Renew **http://hokrenew.com/**

HOK on YouTube **www.youtube.com/user/hoknetwork**

HOK on Facebook **www.facebook.com/HOKCareers**

HOK on Delicious **www.delicious.com/HOKNetwork**

HOK on Flickr **www.flickr.com/photos/hoknetwork/**

HOK on Twitter **http://twitter.com/hoknetwork**

HOK on VisualCV **www.visualcv.com/premier/hok**

HOK on LinkedIn **www.linkedin.com/companies/6624/HOK**

HOK on Slideshare **www.slideshare.net/HOKNetwork**

HOK India Blog **www.hokindia.com/**

Dharavi Evolution **http://dharavievolution.typepad.com/**

Work+Place **www.workplusplace.com/**

The Green Workplace Blog **www.thegreenworkplace.com/**

HOK Canada News **www.hokevents.ca/**

HOK BIM Solutions Blog **http://hokbimsolutions.blogspot.com/**

Life at HOK Feed **http://feeds.feedburner.com/LifeAtHok**

From a positioning perspective, a blog communicates an internal view of the work and the thinking at the firm that can otherwise be difficult to discern.

This exposure, to both prospective clients and talent, offers a real-time commentary that can carry significant credibility for the outsiders looking in.

When it comes to the core social media outlets such as Facebook, LinkedIn, Twitter, Digg, and Plaxo, firms are diving in but as yet uncertain about exactly how to harness the power and possibility they seem to possess. If nothing else, this explosion of connectivity is creating thousands of new micro-communities that largely run under the official radar of most firm leaders. And with so little investment required, every firm needs to determine how to bring this cultural phenomenon into focus, and experiment with its potential. One basic strategy is to find an existing community addressing a topic of high priority for your firm, within a service such as LinkedIn, one of the more neotraditional services in the social media world. Once you're within that community, you can hook up with a Twitter subcommunity that has a focus on that same topic, and gain rapid feedback on ideas you generate. Although Twitter's 140-character limitation doesn't allow for much expansion of the idea, the goal is to get people to a link that tells a story they can react to. Let's say you find a group of 100 folks in the upper Midwest who identify themselves as (1) being in architecture, and (2) being interested in regional sustainability and energy issues. You have an idea that you're considering for a real-world project application related to daylighting, but you're not sure how to measure its effectiveness. You can post your idea and assumptions on your Facebook site or as a link on another site, and Tweet the group with your inquiry and request for assistance. The likelihood is high that you'll receive at least a handful of thoughtful responses, and one of those responses might come from a nearby designer who is willing to share a similar experience or trying to solve the same problem as you are. Either result will be a boost for your effort, and may well result in a string of new connections and sources.

Birds of a feather flock together, and the social media service firms and the marketers who are scouring the sites understand this reality. Another appropriate maxim for this trend is "The friend of your customer is a potential customer." If you haven't explored the world of social media connectivity, perhaps you should, to learn firsthand how these concepts work in a fairly effortless fashion. Let's say you know a marketing director who has a profile on LinkedIn. You go there to review his or her information, and off to the side is a list called "Viewers of this profile also viewed. . . ." This is a come-on to keep you engaged, similar to the filtering and suggesting that occurs on sites such as Amazon. Click on someone you don't know, but who catches your eye—for example, Laurie Schoeman, green building project manager and city planner, in San Francisco. What you might find is one of the more connected individuals on these sites, with an extensive and comprehensive profile, including over 300 connections and a list of groups and organizations that would take a number of hours to fully explore. Her list is copied here to illustrate the point:

- U.S. Green Building Council
- NYPN
- Living Classroom
- Literacy for Environmental Justice
- SF Public Utilities Commission CAC
- GreenBurn
- The Schoeman goils
- United Nations UN-HABITAT
- Capital Green
- Linking Construction
- Water Technologies
- Green Cities
- RFP writing
- Net Zero Energy Buildings
- The-Green-Group.com
- National Association of Home Builders (NAHB)
- Green Professionals
- Clean Technology Job Network
- The RFP Database
- Green Speakers
- Net Zero New York City
- Seven Sisters Alumnae Club
- Water Professionals
- GreenBiz.com—Green Business Professionals
- International Urban Planning & Regional Planning Group
- Sustainable Urban Environmental Infrastructure Professionals
- Green Building
- Green & Sustainability Innovators & Innovation Network
- Forest Stewardship Council and Supporters (FSC)
- Construct IN
- International Professionals

- Smith College Alumnae
- Green Construction, De-Construction, Re-Construction

For those readers who have yet to delve into this type of exploration, it will be worth your time to discover a source that will likely inspire you with a new level of curiosity about these networks. Those of you who have been around this block a few times, or many times every day, know the feeling of finding someone like a Laurie Schoeman whose online reach may suddenly intersect with yours, and well, you send her a message and the conversation begins.

For firms that have yet to approach social media in a formal positioning mode, it's wise to start the process with those on staff who are already engaged in some fashion, as many are likely to be. Get educated about the pros and cons of each service, and the ground rules for interaction. Pick a few topics and interest areas that range across functions including public relations, research, client prospecting, and recruiting. Devise a hierarchy of sites that seem to best fit each of those arenas, and create a small network of people within the firm to get the official ball moving. Be patient, as these communities and networks—while built upon instant communication—can take some time to yield a specific return. One way to help with the process is to make sure the profiles set up on the firm's behalf include the names of specific people, not just the firm name. This can speed up the connection process, and it gives respondents a greater sense of trust when reaching out to the firm. And most certainly, be aware that these tools are intended to build relationships, not to be used to sell a firm's services directly. Practice by responding to the requests and posts of others already on these networks, and that will quickly teach you the ropes of protocol and expectations within this dynamic and evolving world called social media.

Market and Client Research

Once a firm has established its identity, purpose, and overall positioning plan, it's advisable for it to undertake some level of market research annually. Developing a disciplined research regimen will cement the firm's reputation as an expert regarding market trends, deepen competitive intelligence, and generate actionable leads for new work. Research comes in two main categories, primary and secondary, and each contains distinct approaches and value that the firm needs to consider. Many firms will be more comfortable conducting secondary research if they haven't been far down the research road previously. Secondary research is essentially information gathered by third parties, typically including industry and professional associations, government entities, educational institutions, and professional market research firms. The relatively easy access through the Internet drives the value proposition for this approach, since it has the potential of getting the most for the least, in terms of both time and effort. Not all secondary research sources are free, and it's best to work your way up the cost chain to discover the right mix and level of detail you're seeking. Let's say you're an A & E firm looking to assess the Tampa, Florida, market for trends and new opportunities. One place to begin is the following listing of West Central Florida organizations:[1]

Florida Board of Professional Engineers **www.fbpe.org**

Construction Financial Management Association, Tampa Bay Chapter **www.cfmatampabay.org**

Florida Engineering Society - American Institute of Architects **www.fleng.org/**

American Society of Safety Engineers (ASSE) South Florida Chapter **http://southflorida.asse.org/**

University of South Florida, Design Build Program **www.arch.usf.edu/students/sacd_design_build_program/**

Project Management Institute - Tampa Bay Chapter **www.pmi-tampabay.org/index.phtml**

Society of Women Engineers (SWE) Region D - Southeast **http://swe.org/regionD/**

American Institute of Architects - Florida Association **http://aiafla.org//**

Associated Builders and Contractors, Florida Gulf Coast Chapter **www.abcflgulf.org/**

Tampa Chapter of the National Association of Women in Construction **www.nawictampa.org/**

Florida Building Material Association **www.fbma.org**

Florida Transportation Builders' Association **www.ftba.com**

Tampa Bay Builders Association **www.tbba.net**

Each of these sites will provide sources, reports, and additional links to expand your research scope and depth, allowing you to fairly quickly form a snapshot of current and projected activity for the Tampa market. The next set of sources is the publications of the industry you may be

---

[1] List adapted from research developed by Joan Radell of Joanchek Research.

targeting. Get a subscription, order back issues that may focus on specific issues or opportunities of interest, and compile a data sheet that builds a fact-based picture of the market's direction and prospects. At minimum, good secondary research is needed to determine if further time and money should be devoted to primary or original research. A firm that banks on a few select markets for its positioning reputation should have a staggered plan for investing in primary research for each target market.

The first step in designing primary research is to select the research technique that will best meet your goals. While the *observation method* may not seem immediately applicable to the design world, it may well yield results that could draw potential clients closer. If your firm is engaged in retail design, consider a research effort that monitors traffic flow through a retail environment, which could be used to suggest specific design changes to increase sales for a client. If your goal is to be recognized as the retail expert in your region, structure an observation study that can provide evidence-based information for your clients and prospects.

Beyond observation is the *survey method*. Firms that have committed to specialization and market focus are more likely to invest regularly in this technique. Depending on the market, once will not be enough, however. Be ready to repeat the survey every two or three years, to keep it fresh and maintain your position as the firm that clients will rely on to learn about or reaffirm their view of trends. It will be best if you can employ a professional market research firm to conduct and compile survey research. While this increases the investment, it also ensures a more thorough approach, plus state-of-the-art analysis and presentation of data that can mean a stronger payoff for the firm's positioning program.

For client research, as opposed to market research, the firm may under-take more of a do-it-yourself approach. Often, firms use client surveys to gain feedback on previous jobs, seek out ideas for new services, or work on improving various operational aspects. The nature of these topics makes it more critical that a design professional construct and interpret the questions and resulting data, lessening the value of a third party in the process.

Another valuable research tool available to design firms (and not em-ployed often enough), is the use of *focus groups*. For firms with a clear vision of their direction, focus groups are the perfect forum for gaining insight from clients and prospects while "practicing" their position as thought-leading ex-perts. Any practice group or market leader that goes through a 12-month period without conducting at least one focus group session is missing a most valuable source of information, and will likely be surpassed by a dif-ferent firm's expert, sooner rather than later. The structure of focus groups can vary based on the complexity of the topic, the number of participants, and the firm's ultimate goals, but their value is clear. Focus groups are a powerful tool for ascertaining interest in future or abstract concepts the firm may be considering. The negative aspect of these groups is that it's best to use a short survey to feed the process before it begins, or to provide some reading for the participants to complete beforehand. Those activities, combined with the two to three hours of actual group discussion, mean that participants will need to be highly motivated in order to commit. Cost can also be a minor concern, as it's often considered best to utilize an outside facilitator, unless someone in the firm can truly take a neutral position in moving the process through its stages. Obviously, given the small numbers in a focus group environment, there will be a lack of hard data at the conclusion. This means that your up-front selection process needs to be very strong, ensuring that the participants are already interested in the topic at hand, active in their roles of exploring or promoting the topic, and expressive enough to make a meaningful contribution in a short time period.

This chapter began with an emphasis on the term "system" as the vital aspect required to ensure success in positioning through the core marketing elements. Excellence in marketing, and hence positioning, is a matter of synergy. It requires a series of logical hand-offs and connections that need to occur within the firm's operations, span known networks, and penetrate into the lesser-known realms of social media. Despite the randomness of some of these activities, a firm's positioning platform can be communicated on a clear and consistent basis, and staff can be coached to understand the nuances of what's most important to the firm. To leave the marketing process at the traditional core while so much activity and connectivity is happening at the edge is a mistake that many firms will make, and they will regret the time they have lost. Firm leaders who grasp the salient aspects of the Big Shift, along with the generational hand-off that is occurring, will not only find themselves better prepared for the changes ahead, they will actually enjoy the ride . . . perhaps immensely.

METHODS BUYERS ARE USING TO PROCURE SERVICES

To gain some additional perspective on the entire discussion of marketing, consider a recent survey of buyers that identifies and ranks their primary sources for learning about professional services providers. What's not surprising is that most introductions are made via traditional means such as referrals or other personal connections or exposure. It's noteworthy that 2 of the top 10 sources weren't even around 15 years ago, namely websites and Internet searches. Podcasts, social media, and blogs are way down at the bottom of the list, but don't discount their potential and future effects. For the full rundown, see the chart in Figure 5.4.

It may still be a few more years before people who are looking to build a $50 million facility will admit that they found out about the designer through a Tweet, but you never know—stranger things have happened!

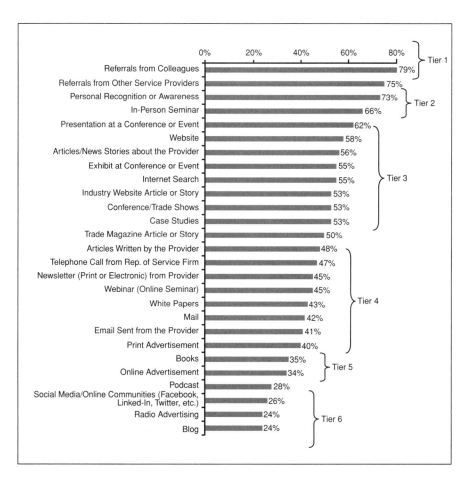

Figure 5.4 Although many buying habits of clients are fairly predictable, the new competitive landscape, along with new social media tools, is disrupting what's defined as "normal." (*Source:* Authors Mike Schultz and John Doerr, RainToday.com, Figure 3.1, pg. 22, *How Clients Buy: 2009 Benchmark Report,* 2009)

CHAPTER **6**

ORGANIZATIONAL DEVELOPMENT

When leaders understand the power, purpose, and necessity of on-going organizational development (OD) as a key ingredient for firm success, the topic is always at or near the top of their list of priorities. Unfortunately, much of the design industry has been woefully weak in valuing this process, and pays the price year after year. Project management skills are highly valued as a discipline, but they often involve a firefighting approach that doesn't include learning from repetitive mistakes; hence, the organization doesn't develop. In addition, many leaders look only as far as the project level when assessing organizational performance, leaving the larger issues and opportunities untouched and unrealized. Organizations that see themselves as learning and growing organisms know that OD works in two directions: from the micro out, which starts from a task- and project-based position, and from the macro in, which starts with overall organizational design. This approach helps ensure that the firm is creating productive tension between what they need to do today, and where they are heading in the longer term. In order to get there, the firm needs a good design to guide the way. Grounding a firm in the core principles of organizational design requires an understanding of the following four important elements.

- Alignment
- Accountability

- Interdependency
- Change management

Alignment within a firm begins with a clear vision and vector. The firm knows who they are, what their purpose is, and how these essentials inform their ultimate goals. A firm that is well aligned has a unified marketing system in place that serves the needs of all studios, principals, divisions, and branches. Valuing alignment helps to manage the "creep" of individual decisions that can render an important function useless. An example of this is the contradiction associated with staff performance reviews. Although most leaders understand the importance and usefulness of such systems, they are often either ignored or applied in an indiscriminate fashion. An aligned firm develops an appropriate review process, trains its supervisors on how to apply it, and carefully monitors the ongoing implementation. Leaders responsible for the process periodically read up on new ideas, and will call in outside expertise promptly to help design a new system when the current approach becomes ineffective. The entire array of considerations—from strategy to firm policy, and from pricing to staff scheduling—requires the same level of alignment. A firm can grow only when there is clarity on these issues, and all responsible parties are willing to march in the same direction.

Accountability within a firm begins with the recognition that defining the roles and responsibilities of all key processes, functions, and systems is critically important to the health of the firm. In an industry filled with professional self-interest and individual achievement, the leaning tends to be toward "accountability for my projects and clients," often leaving precious little time and energy to apply to the good of the overall firm. Accountability requires adherence to procedures, policies, and decision-making criteria, even when there seems to be a good rationale to declare an exception. In many firms, those exceptions never end, and so the accountability factor shrinks. Such problems can occur when the firm is seeking to develop its design reputation. For example, suppose the decision is made to open up the design concept stage to a broader internal audience, promoting a variety of new ideas, feedback, and the feeling of a more collaborative environment. Yet as time passes, principals begin avoiding the process, wanting to keep the opportunity to themselves, at great expense to less experienced staff who need the opportunity to contribute to the entire design-creation process. Firms that manage this dynamic well are able to establish a value system that celebrates effort for the good of all, while still leaving room for individual accomplishment and recognition. Accountability is also a function of clear roles and responsibilities designed to induce a strong sense of seriousness of purpose.

Interdependency within a firm begins with the accountability principle, and adds the dimension of connectivity to others in the firm and to the firm's clients, networks, and service partners. The interdependency principle is grounded in respect and trust, and is the glue that each organization needs to stay unified. Those who understand how this principle operates can skillfully navigate around personality issues and even principled disagreements by keeping the focus on the value of processes and the need for systems integrity in running the firm. While exceptions are always made for the right situation, staff come to understand that another version of today's excuse for not following a required procedure just won't cut it. Healthy interdependency recognizes the vital need for all participants to comply with the rules. One of the most common (and expensive) ways this principle is violated concerns project scope management. Too often, scope management begins with the proposal and contract, finds its way down the river of client changes, value engineering, and subcontractor error, and ends up at the mouth of the Gulf of Lawsuits and Claims. Many firms lose a tremendous amount of revenue and profit when scope decisions either aren't exposed, or are dealt with in an after-the-fact, defensive manner. Client appeasement should be a small, inexpensive item, not a $50,000 write-off that subverts open discussion and a rational decision-making process that respects the reality of interdependency within the firm.

Change management begins with the knowledge that change is not only necessary, it's also a good thing. A firm that is committed to systems development of key functions finds that change is easier for them than for a firm that wings its way through the decades, establishing a string of temporary fixes that come and go without serious contemplation. Leaders need a buffer of logic to effectively execute transformational change, and this logic is derived from the ability to clearly describe where the firm has been and what the picture of the future looks like, all communicated in a systems-oriented language. The smartest leaders understand that their firm is fully connected to the external world, and when that world moves, they need to make adjustments. They apply the principles of alignment, accountability, and interdependency when designing the changes needed, thereby smoothing the way for acceptance and efficiency. This approach avoids the traditional trap of managing change through endless negotiations with resistors who only want to stay put. The most effective change management occurs when firms develop a head of steam around a new philosophy or purpose. Instead of continuing to rely on projects as the source of inspiration, they design bold new ideas about the firm itself to raise their staffs' eyes and minds skyward. Instead of fighting numerous individual battles about the details of making incremental change, they let the world and their markets inform them of the new direction they need to follow. In other words, change management should only be approached from a positive perspective, not as the way to fix everything that's not working. Leaders who understand how organizations function know that the lower-level problems within the firm have a much greater chance of being addressed if the firm has been able to paint a picture of a compelling future. Instead of arranging a heavy-handed scrutiny of document quality, they'll implement a two-year initiative to promote cross-training and tie it to a more aggressive schedule for professional registrations and other meaningful certifications. Those who refuse to respond to the program, whose work continues to exhibit quality weaknesses, will then be counseled and separated from the firm as necessary. Handling it this way allows the firm to fix the problems at hand while simultaneously reaching for higher ground, thereby keeping the mindset among the majority of staff positive and forward-looking.

Leaders who follow these principles of organizational design reach a point where consistency, applied within a complex environment, is rewarded with much greater control over the ship. Although every organization needs to take care when heading off to new horizons, those that learn and follow these important principles will have much greater—if not complete—confidence in making the journey successfully.

PRIMARY ARENAS FOR ORGANIZATIONAL DEVELOPMENT

When a firm is looking to advance its competence in organizational development, four arenas emerge as the most vital sources for progress. These sources are:

- Infrastructure development
- Leadership development
- Organizational life cycles
- Learning systems

Exploration of each of these arenas provides firm leaders with a well-rounded array of topics to keep under consideration as their organization grows, matures, and faces both expected and unexpected ups and downs.

Infrastructure Development

Facility design is ultimately a collection of complex tasks organized to achieve the goal of building a quality product for a client. This is also the case when building an organization—we begin with essential tasks, and look to leverage that effort to a point where the value of the whole exceeds its parts. The tasks involved in running a design firm would be overwhelming if not organized into processes, namely the procedures necessary to organize the tasks. Once the processes begin to develop, a function emerges, and it's at this stage that many firms look to apply a dedicated resource to control and manage this function. If we think of the realm of proposal development and other basic marketing functions, the picture becomes clearer. Many firms begin with founders writing their own proposals from beginning to end. Once they have accumulated enough baseline materials, they begin to collaborate with other principals, eventually establishing a process for proposal production. Once the number of proposals and the amount of effort required exceed a certain level, they will hire a marketing coordinator to produce the bulk of the work, leaving them to define the flavor and story angles that every proposal needs to be distinctive. If the firm continues to grow steadily, they will establish a marketing manager position to design and produce additional materials and approaches to get the word out about the firm. And for many firms, this "function" level—where a department is now staffed by two levels of resources—is where they get stuck. The number one reason for getting stuck is the belief that all non-design staff are overhead, an attitude that does not encourage them to focus on achieving or maintaining profitability. Second, there is also a lack of appreciation for the value of the two remaining levels in the hierarchy, the system level and the integrated platform. See Figure 6.1.

The system level receives a more positive reception when the firm shifts from viewing proposal development as "my workload" to a greater sense of the competitive advantage that can be derived from additional investment in the process. At the system level, this process is no longer just a proposal production machine; it becomes part of a much larger marketing system. This new definition of purpose allows the responsible staff to expand their thinking around their ultimate purpose, and the firm can then begin to march forward. When we set a higher target to aim at, we become more focused on establishing a smoothly running system for the lower half of the marketing production infrastructure, namely the production of proposals. As we add on the top half of the system, we take on new thoughts about how to influence clients using proposals, how to extend our thinking about the use of models and visuals to enhance the words, and how to make our proposals a true competitive advantage. This new freedom from the grips of production (lower level tasks) allows us to conduct research with clients about which types and aspects of proposals work best for them, and learn about our competitors' state of the art.

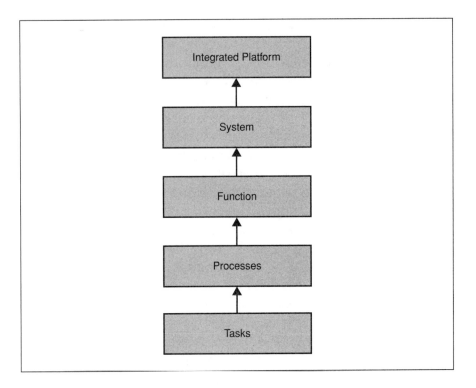

Figure 6.1 The development of a strong and well-aligned firm infrastructure requires a systems viewpoint in order to succeed. Simply adding on new tasks to address current issues usually results in more confusion down the road. (*Source:* SPARKS, The Center for Strategic Planning)

At the integrated platform level, another important change occurs. We create connectivity to the art of the presentation, now seeing a clearer purpose in the realm of client persuasion. Building on this new relationship between proposals and presentations, we can no longer value only basic production measurements. How we measure ourselves changes, and this entire process puts positive pressure on key individuals to step up to new standards of performance. Along the way, we may also discover the need to hire an additional marketing coordinator or two, and upgrade the head of marketing to director or chief marketing officer. We continue to make investments in this department, and begin to measure its value in new ways—not just as an overhead expense based on production-style performance.

Adding management muscle and systems-oriented skills to a firm is liable to include the addition of the chief operating officer position. Such a position can have tremendous influence on the inner workings of a firm, increasing efficiency, accountability, and overall performance. Consider the experience of a mid-sized firm in Central New York, in the following case study.

CASE STUDY: ASHLEY MCGRAW ARCHITECTS, SYRACUSE, NEW YORK

CREATING THE COO POSITION IN A GROWING ARCHITECTURAL PRACTICE

Deborah Rhea isn't one to sit idly around, looking for something to do. Her career has spanned a wide scope of organizations and responsibilities, including stints in the private sector, government, and academia. With an MBA in finance, and a PhD in the leadership of higher education, she's now in her third year as the chief operating and finance officer for Ashley McGraw Architects in Syracuse, New York. With a staff of 75, the firm has seen explosive growth in the past four years, more than doubling total staff in that timeframe.

According to Ed McGraw, CEO of the firm, "Even though Deborah didn't have professional services experience, we knew from the first interview that she was just what we needed." He goes on to explain that they were a firm that needed greater efficiency and operational controls in order to meet their full potential and, frankly, increase their profitability.

Deborah was up to the challenge. She dug in with the senior staff to understand what they were doing with their time, and how they could be more productive when it came to operations. What followed was a thorough revamping of the organization, with the relinquishment of many project management responsibilities by the principals to a newly formalized level of project managers. The firm expanded its operations support with the addition of a project information manager, a staff of project coordinators, an administrative assistant to the principals and the COO/CFO, a specifications technician, and additional IT staff to upgrade and manage systems. What is typically anathema to a design firm (the addition of overhead personnel) has resulted in overwhelming success for the firm. According to Ed and the other principals, they took the risk, and it paid off in spades.

Deborah explains how her diverse skills and perspective helped make this possible. She says, "Having run organizations in a variety of sectors and variety of sizes and types, I could easily see both the unique and common aspects of an architectural design firm. At the point I joined the firm, Ashley McGraw Architects had reached the point in its development where it was appropriate to separate the business of architecture from the production of architectural design. Stripping away operations and the administrative aspects of project management from the Partners and Project Managers allowed them to concentrate on design and client development while simultaneously strengthening the administrative support capacities of the firm. The efficiency of relinquishing operational and project administration tasks to administrative experts is reflected in the 45% increase in revenues during the last three years, while maintaining consistent direct and indirect costs to revenue ratios. Overhead continues to be 20% of revenues."

The result has been a complete conversion in the thinking of those who weren't sure of the need to bring in high-priced talent to address these kinds of problems. According to Nick Signorelli, firm principal and head of the K–12 studio, "I wasn't too sure for quite a while how this decision would turn out. But, I also knew we needed to make some changes about how we managed our time and our roles. In the end, things are much different for me because of what's developed since Deborah's arrival. I'm a better leader, a better designer and I can devote my time to where it's really needed. The support we now have in the studios is more valuable than I can measure."

What other benefits have accrued from this bold move? According to Deborah, "Every organization benefits from streamlining its production processes and standardizing repetitive tasks. Contrary to quashing design creativity, the imposition of production policies and the establishment of clearly defined reporting lines have allowed the designers to spend more time on design innovation, and the partners in business development."

What other concerns did the staff have when this initiative was starting? There was concern over a loss of the "cultural cohesion" that had been developed within and among the studios. People were naturally comfortable with the status quo, and the idea of an outsider coming in to make changes was unsettling, to say the least. As Deborah sees it, it took someone from outside the world of architecture to push the boundaries of what's possible for the organization to achieve.

And how does she see the future, now that the first few years have gone so well? "The firm's commitment to sustainable design has positioned it well for continued success. It is very gratifying to me to work in this intellectually and artistically progressive environment. Adapting conventional management and business practices to accommodate an inherently anti-bureaucratic culture is both challenging and rewarding."

She's also focused on the talent side of the business. A big part of Deborah's efforts since joining Ashley McGraw has been recruiting new employees. She finds she can tell the Ashley McGraw story from a different angle, and it generates interest among potential staff members, service partners, and clients. "We've professionalized our approach to running this very creative business in a very business-like way. Potential employees are intrigued by the firm's sustainable design initiatives and its merit-based assignment and promotion system. The firm's ability to represent itself well to applicants has enabled us to attract and hire top-notch talent from around the world."

The bottom line is that the addition of key strategic roles can have a great effect on the leadership, the entire staff, and the firm's results. What might have been considered a questionable addition of overhead is now integral to the firm's success and future capabilities. Perhaps Ed McGraw sums it up best when he says: "Without Deborah here, my life would be very, very different. I can now spend time really looking ahead for the firm, and working with the principals and other key staff on initiatives that will keep us vibrant, healthy and ahead of the pack. It's great to know the firm is operating so well, and Deborah is a huge part of that reason. I simply can't imagine going back to how we were operating a few short years ago."

Once a firm has reached the level of developing an integrated platform (which obviously includes more than just proposals and presentations), the firm leaders will understand that the expense/investment side of the equation has accomplished two huge goals. It has developed the kind of leadership and capabilities that allow it to compete for better projects over wider territories, and it has weeded out those staff members who, while valued for their basic skills, couldn't help the firm climb the next mountain. So, in the end, striving for the top of the hierarchy signifies not only achievement but also a necessary cleansing—a refreshment of the standards of performance that are needed to keep a competitive edge and ascend the ladder of recognition and accomplishment. This concept helps explain why spending a bundle of money on new IT systems or software can wind up as a wasteful exercise for some firms. Leaders must be prepared not only to purchase the latest tools, but also to challenge people as a consequence of that decision and action. In some cases, these repercussions can alter long-held relationships and associations, especially if the firm has allowed too much leeway regarding buy-in and commitment to new ways of working. When a firm's OD has reached a point where opting out of significant changes is no longer acceptable, these new initiatives can be more fully realized and valued as an important step in the firm's continual development.

LEADERSHIP DEVELOPMENT

The most effective leadership development cycle occurs when combining a careful redesign of the organization with new strategy and positioning goals. These goals might include a refinement or reassertion of values, new performance initiatives such as greater operational efficiency, new positioning programs such as firm branding, or a major push into the thought leadership front lines of a high-priority client market. The attempt to climb new mountains with old equipment—including a worn and unimaginative organization structure—isn't likely to succeed.

One rule of thumb for understanding when a new leadership approach is needed is to think of the moment when the founder or CEO of a firm can no longer invite everyone to dinner and seat them all at one table. The second, correlated criterion for this moment of change is that those at one end of the table can't hear what's being said at the other end. Picture this effect cascading down through a complex, growing organization, and the resulting picture suggests that it's very easy to fall behind in the advancement of effective leadership development. As with many industries, the design profession falls prey to the Peter Principle, (Laurence J. Peter, *The Peter Principle*, Raymond Hull, 1969), the theory that all somewhat ambitious individuals will be promoted to at least one level above their actual competency, and remain in place thereafter, as a daily reminder that the organization really doesn't know what it's doing! That particular image aside, the exploration of the leadership development arena needs to start with the three most vital and essential characteristics for firm leaders.

The "Vital Three" for Leaders:

- Vision formulation
- Ambition
- Execution skills

From a positioning perspective, leaders and their leadership capabilities are the critical drivers that both define and create the results achieved. With vision as the definition of a meaningful goal, and execution as the work required to navigate the journey, it's ambition that holds the entire process together, overcoming obstacles and keeping the engine of the firm humming and well fueled.

True leadership means modeling the behaviors necessary to inspire others, and doing so with humility. In most industries, leadership is conceived of as a matter of control, and of driving others to bend to the leader's will. Professional services generally offer a less dramatic version of the leadership role, but leaders in these fields still have much to learn about how to lead effectively. Leadership that stems primarily from title or from the position of founder or principal still needs to be tested, proven, and expanded. Titles don't protect anyone from having to meet their responsibilities head-on, and even the founder of a firm will need to explain positions and decisions in the face of earnest questions. For many in design firms, the apex is ownership, and with that status comes the temptation to perpetuate a particular leadership style, instead of monitoring how external conditions demand new thinking and behaviors from current and future leaders. This condition can reduce the energy that comes with ambition, robbing the firm of future opportunities for important advances. An additional complication emerges when it becomes obvious that an owner/partner not only lacks drive and ambition, but is actually an obstacle to progress. For this reason, firms may want to consider a more formal separation of ownership and leadership, thereby eliminating the requirement to impose executive responsibilities on anyone who happens to be a shareholder.

Building a program to assess and develop stronger leadership skills usually requires external assistance, but the process can begin with two excellent books: *The Leadership Challenge*, by Jim Kouzes and Barry Posner, and *On Becoming a Leader*, by Warren Bennis. *The Leadership Challenge Workbook* offers exercises and discussion guides to enhance the reading. It includes Five Practices of exemplary leadership:

- Model the way.
- Inspire a shared vision.
- Challenge the process.
- Enable others to act.
- Encourage the heart.

Additionally, every firm leader should be reading *Business Week* and *The Harvard Business Review* to keep current on corporate examples and macro business ideas and trends occurring outside the design world. The first task for many leaders who are interested in strengthening these Five Practices is to create the space to do so. Leaders who are more concerned about their billable time and direct project involvement are making a trade-off that exacts a deeper price than their monthly billings can compensate for.

Once you've selected the leadership characteristics that resonate for you or your firm, and have done some reading, the next step is to engage in a leadership development program. A simple five-step program culminating in an individual development plan (IDP) would include the following components:

- Write down your professional aspirations and goals, setting a time-frame for expected achievement. These should number about four or five in total, and be able to fit on half a page. Include items that concern you as an individual, plus those that will coincidentally advance the firm.

- Describe your current leadership/management responsibilities. This should be done in some detail, by thinking through the actual level of responsibility you carry for end results, not just your involvement in a variety of functions. This should be recorded in one or two pages.

- List the additional roles and opportunities you see for yourself and the firm. For yourself, tack back to your professional aspirations, and begin to calculate the value of your potential contributions to the firm when and if the time becomes available to pursue them. Certain opportunities for the firm may not necessarily involve your IDP, but can be discussed by the entire leadership team as you seek to identify voids and weaknesses that need to be filled. Put these ideas on one or two pages.

- Conduct a use-of-time analysis, utilizing the guide in Table 6-1. Add other elements to the current or future view, as needed. When entering current time percent, be sure to base it on the past 6–12 months, as opposed to shorter timeframes. The "New challenge" and "New role" line items may not be currently active, but including them as future time allocations begins to set up the necessary decisions for making significant shifts in your role.

- Describe the obstacles to the achievement of your goals. You cannot use "time" or "cost" as an obstacle. The idea is to get to the essence

TABLE 6-1: Use-of-Time Analysis

Area of Responsibility	Current %	Future %
Design		
Marketing		
Project management		
Financial matters		
Other business affairs		
Client relations		
Training/mentoring		
New challenge		
New role		

of what you want to achieve, and then match that with where the firm is headed. Summarize the actions you'll take, the timeframes, and other important elements, and gain agreement from other leaders. Be sure to note how each new role or new time allocation is connected to an important strategic or positioning goal, and decide how this will be communicated within the firm. Some items may be able to start immediately, while others will require a smooth transition. The important thing is to develop a plan that's interconnected in all directions: one that works for the leader, works for the leadership team, and works for the entire firm.

Once a leadership team has constructed these individual plans and linked them to the needs of the firm, there should be a formal communication to the staff. Logically, this would represent an implementation phase for a previously announced vision or direction. By modeling this logic and connectivity, the firm will send the message that it's serious about the future, and that the leaders are making personal investments in change, in order to realize the desired results. With this investment in the bank, resistors within the ranks will have nowhere to hide, and dealing with such obstacles will be much easier when the time comes.

With the leadership development plans in hand and fully announced, it's wise to conduct brief reviews every three months or so, to assess status and progress. Addressing the murky topic of leadership development can be a real challenge, but when combined with an inspiring set of goals for the firm, the process will quickly offer new, valuable perspectives on what it takes to achieve those goals.

Influence of Firm Size on Leadership Behaviors and Requirements

The general responsibilities of leaders are fairly consistent, regardless of firm size, but some important distinctions should be made across the spectrum. For a small firm (up to 50 in total staff), assume that five principals are on board, which includes two founders. In this model, the founders will be viewed as autocrats, whether they particularly exhibit those characteristics or not. Small firms are run with an air of deference to founders, sometimes to the great frustration of other principals who weren't there from Day One. The level of project involvement of these leaders will often be quite high, and while that can help in client relations and marketing, it tends to stifle the development of second- and third-tier staff. Most leadership in these situations occurs as technical directives, and there's a danger that this phenomenon can create a factory-style environment, suppressing good ideas and inhibiting the development of promising talent. If at least one of the founders has a strong entrepreneurial streak that extends beyond the founding of the firm, he or she can generate more excitement and possibility. New ideas will keep other principals and younger staff thinking about the future, and how they might develop a more important role, perhaps with a new design approach or a deeper service to an important market. One of the greatest long-term challenges for a small firm is how to identify and resolve project and client problems at a level below the founder(s). Once the bad habit of letting all issues rise to the top has taken hold, reversing that flow can be difficult. Senior PMs who have been at the firm for over five years may also feel at risk if they're told to step in and address issues that have typically been handled by the top echelon. They may believe that if a misstep is made, another opportunity to take on greater responsibilities might be a long time in coming. And of course, the leaders often don't want to let go of the issue to begin with. The way to address this problem is to start small. Instead of issuing a sweeping directive that tries to reverse the old habits all at once, pick the two strongest PMs and one principal to form a team that can make consultative decisions on issues as they arise. Once agreement is reached, it's down to a matter of implementation, and in this way, exposure can be limited while still moving in a more productive direction. Perhaps the topics that fall to this new level should be limited to design, technical, and general administrative issues, allowing contract and financial matters to continue to receive executive/founder consideration. This team approach will take a bit longer, but the learning will still be accomplished. The trick with this approach is to be able to transfer actual responsibility, which can be quite difficult for some leaders to imagine after 30 years of managing their clients personally. It must be done, however, or the organization will flounder as younger staff stop developing, and the senior level starts to think about slowing down or retiring.

For the medium-sized firm of up to 150 staff, the entire leadership concept has typically developed more serious traction. Once a firm has upwards of 10–15 principals, a fully developed infrastructure, and fully functional departments staffed with multiple levels of talent, there is no choice but to have some form of leadership development program in place. The real question becomes: "What are the criteria used to select and promote staff into higher-level positions, and does this process align with the long-term vision of the firm's direction?" Medium-sized firms will have reasonably well defined processes, functions, and systems, each requiring periodic review, improvement, and expansion. Leaders at all levels of the firm can be assigned ownership for these components, and numerous virtual teams can be established to manage the issues and opportunities that arise, often on a temporary project basis. These firms will also have added positions such as chief operating officer, chief financial officer, and chief marketing officer, to assist in the management of the enterprise. It's important that those filling these positions exhibit strong interpersonal skills as well as the technical capabilities to fill the post. When designed correctly, these positions will find ways to lighten the load of the project-driven professional staff so they can dedicate more time to project and client needs, not administrative and "corporate" demands. However, one important distinction is that these "C-suite" positions should not be held responsible for end results that must be achieved by other principals, project staff, market/studio leaders, and the like. It can be tempting to think that the new CMO should have a $1 million revenue quota for the year, but in reality, CMOs should be master facilitators of positioning for revenue, not of getting contracts signed. The same goes for the COO. While it might seem logical to let the COO figure out and execute an entire operational improvement program, including bringing home the bacon with a final report of huge cost savings, the fact is that those initiatives must be accomplished by embedding new processes and approaches into the work of the project staff. With a full-fledged executive team in place, a medium-sized firm can become a real powerhouse in their chosen markets. On the other hand, a firm that thinks that all that overhead is risky or wasteful usually winds up with a raft of problems. Growing to a size of 110 in staff without the systems-oriented formalized leadership positions in place usually means the firm will crater as soon as the current influx of work has dropped off. One common signal of this problem is hiring many new faces without holding an orientation session or making introductions, so that six months later the newcomers still don't know which end is up. This lack of infrastructure development will keep the firm inefficient, reducing profits. New systems and software won't be understood or used to their full benefit, wasting capital and time. Each division or studio will continue to do things its own way, leaving the firm without a unified image, message, and purpose in the marketplace. Lastly, firms that don't develop real leaders with significant responsibilities and opportunities will allow their best talent to walk out the door. It's one thing to gain valuable project experience at a busy, bustling firm, and another thing entirely to envision the multiple layers of your career that can blossom there, supported by real evidence of those whose careers have done just that in a previous phase.

For the larger firms, many of these dynamics change once again. Firms with numerous offices of 100 staff each are now run in a more corporate fashion. Decisions related to systems, processes, policies, and the like tend to arrive unannounced, or without much local input. The projects are bigger, the clients more prestigious, and that can mean a lot to the professionals on the team. There's important work being done, more media are showing up for interviews today, and a movie on the founder's life is in postproduction. This can create the impression that the firm is unassailable and will succeed forever. Yet, behind the name, notoriety, and multitude of success stories is a rigidity that takes a toll, as 10-year veterans will find when they do an honest inventory of the satisfiers they expected at that stage. Opportunities to move up are certainly there, but competition is fierce, and loyalties can shift like the wind. Politics are much more a part of the career now, and the freedom of creating their own influential design expressions may have become a distant memory. The challenge for leaders in these firms is to hire the right talent and then work hard to keep them informed, motivated, and inspired. Smaller firms can offer a less structured approach to giving a staff member freedom to explore or develop something new. A large firm needs to sanction these opportunities in a more formal, programmatic fashion, perhaps by creating a new division to explore a potentially profitable new market. New staff entering a larger firm may desire to be connected with the greater exposure and impact the final product will have, but they need to have a temperament that can abide having less control over their work. Perhaps it's similar to the difference between playing baseball in Kansas City and playing in New York or Boston. Even some great players can't deal with the expectations and pressure of a big-city team, and need to go where they feel that more relaxed "family" connection again.

Each of these versions of leadership is valid and necessary, and each requires that a new twist be applied to the same basic concepts and principles. For a firm of any size, any age, and any particular set of goals and aspirations, the real questions are: "Are you consciously building a leadership style and approach that strengthen the firm and its people, and position you for all that the future will offer? Are you avoiding the pitfalls of choosing friendship with one over progress for many? Are you modeling a leadership style that is well balanced and presenting new challenges even after 25 years at the helm?" And lastly: "Are you willing to risk leaving your own comfort zones in order to give the next generation the opportunity to seize upon their own definition of the future, allowing them the chance to succeed against conditions and competitors none of us has yet faced?"

The Entrepreneurial Leader

Entrepreneurial skills are also a topic deserving attention when it comes to the question of leadership. Not all firms are entrepreneurial in culture, and this can't be considered a "must" for every leader, but it surely has its place. Entrepreneurs are those who apply a dynamic combination of additional skills to the business of design. They evoke a spirit that many people find infectious. They are typically innovative and creative in their approach to opportunities, and often create an opportunity where no evidence of one existed. The mindset of an entrepreneur is one that's full of possibilities, and one that strongly discounts the obstacles that would thwart the average leader. An entrepreneur isn't prone to dealing with situations in a blunt manner, neither demanding nor cajoling like a salesman to accomplish his goal. More intuitive than most, entrepreneurs work around the edges of a perceived opportunity, collecting and assessing diverse sets of information as they begin to draw a mental picture of how to become the force that brings seemingly disconnected elements into a whole. A common misconception about entrepreneurs is that they are risk takers. While they are comfortable with the unknown, they are in fact excellent risk assessors. Successful entrepreneurs don't take uncalculated risks; they move in a direction that's been plotted out from the discoveries they've made about a client, about a market, or about potential synergy others aren't paying attention to. Steve Einhorn of EYP may be the best example of an entrepreneur when it comes to the design industry. Highly aware, highly perceptive, aggressive, and confident, he was a great business mind well before most design firms knew that business was required reading. He built and managed EYP to become a well-oiled machine that delivered excellence in design services while functioning internally as his own version of IBM. The leaders communicated like people who were in fact running an important enterprise, not a practice that dabbled in a version of applied artistry. Perhaps the pinnacle of his achievement of blending design and business was the creation and ultimate sale of EYP Mission Critical Facilities, Inc. to Hewlett-Packard in 2007. While most firms would assume that the IT industry had all the bases covered when it came to data centers, Einhorn discovered that they didn't—and pounced. EYP found and filled a void in the system that others were lazily assuming wasn't design industry turf; in the process, Einhorn solved some significant problems for his clients, and then he sold the enterprise for a sizable sum of money. His achievement would be very hard to duplicate, but as a model for how entrepreneurs view the world and take action, it rings true every day of the week.

Some additional characteristics associated with entrepreneurs include:

- Focus
- Persistence
- Passion
- Flexibility
- Optimism
- Creative thinking
- Persuasion
- Goal setting

Taken together, all the important characteristics of leaders listed in this section begin to paint a picture that can become the baseline requirements for a firm. Many times, leaders are chosen for technical, design, or project management skills, which are necessary but not sufficient for the type of leadership that will make the firm the best it can be. Not every leader will possess all of the skills included here, but every team should strive to have these skills represented among them as a group.

THE LEARNING ENVIRONMENT

Knowledge management has been espoused as a central aspect of organizational learning in the design industry over the past 15 years. Unfortunately, most of this effort has been at the fairly low level of information sharing, and

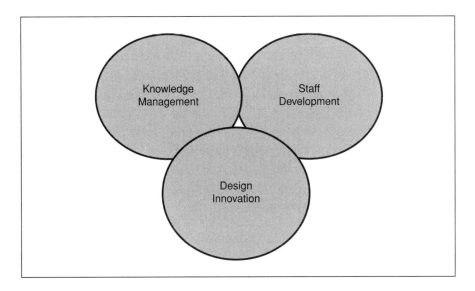

Figure 6.2   This model represents the learning system that is needed in firms. Integrating knowledge flows and sources with staff development is key to achieving higher levels of design innovation. (*Source:* SPARKS, The Center for Strategic Planning)

while that process is important, it's hardly the whole story. Larger aspects of knowledge management and learning are more complex, create more demands, and have greater payoffs when achieved. Learning within design firms should be systematized and formalized to create the palpable sense that learning is important—that it is a driver for the firm's culture and values. The model for a learning environment is shown in Figure 6.2.

The progressive interaction of these three components of the learning environment offers important navigational tools for a firm seeking stronger positioning as a technical, design, or market expert. In fact, these components are critical to the very survival of most firms that see the design firm of the future as a "one-stop shop" for client needs. Let's begin with knowledge management. Information sharing is its basic starting point; it then graduates to the level of analysis. Information sharing is based on the flow of projects through the firm, and while that flow provides a relatively small amount of knowledge, it's usually enough to build on. Let's assume the firm has taken an interest in the senior housing market, and has three or four projects under its belt. Many firms will use standard networking skills to search out more of the same, and if they're lucky, those new projects will materialize. However, sooner or later, the networking source will run dry, and in most cases that will mean the firm moves on to other project types. As a result, the firm is busy enough to be considered successful, but they lack the leverage to make things happen based on their level of expanded expertise. For the firm that wants to go deeper into the market and influence it from the design perspective, more steps are needed. The second and third steps include technical and market analysis for senior housing, based both on the projects executed and on what can be discovered through primary and secondary research. This analysis might reveal two or three emerging technologies that cross over from the medical field, and perhaps a new set of demographic data that shows important trends within various regions of the country. Putting these elements in combination, the firm can then embark on the process of developing trends and making modest attempts at predicting the market's direction over time.

Coincident with the knowledge management evolution just described, a focused effort needs to be underway in relation to staff development. Some of the first stage could be the product of one individual, but that's not the most desirable situation. The firm needs to be engaging others in the process, exposing them to some of the questions that need to be answered, and orienting them as to how the senior housing market has developed over the recent years. Within this context, the firm should formalize certain roles and responsibilities around knowledge management and research, and assign specific goals to be accomplished. Assuming that this process now includes a number of staff members, leadership responsibilities can be divided into a few camps. These might include thought leadership about how the basic concepts of the market have developed and how the future direction is shaping up. Technical leadership around the issues and technology related to the medical aspects is another possible role. In the end, the goal is to involve more people in the process of learning about the market, and to divide their responsibilities in a way that will cause greater depths to be plumbed as time passes.

Lastly, there's the design innovation aspect. How do we take the technical, market, and trends information and make it a function of design? It happens by formalizing a design innovation effort tied to the senior housing market, with a goal of creating an innovation conduit that will feed the next set of projects the firm brings in. This process begins with picking the one or two most promising aspects of design that this market represents. For the moment, let's consider them to be food service/dining and inpatient psychological counseling. Both areas are always seeking advancement and new ideas, and a great variety of approaches can be drawn from other settings in the broader worlds of healthcare, counseling, university campuses, and so forth. The idea is to build the questions and the effort internally, and take the firm beyond the specifics of the three or four actual projects performed. A market expert looking for a position of influence within the client industry will dig deeper, ask more questions, and provide greater perspective than the other firms down the road that might also want a slice of the senior housing pie—and this capability starts with creating a learning environment that will attract and challenge the staff beyond today's immediate tasks.

FIRM VALUES

Words carry weight, and every firm has the opportunity to make its words count for more. Whether this effort begins with individual leaders carrying out their daily responsibilities, or with a more formalized approach to consciously raising the importance of what's said, simple words make an enormous difference. Fernando Flores, a PhD from University of California at Berkeley and former minister of finance in Chile, co-authored a seminal book on human cognition and artificial intelligence, and is best known for his research into organizational behavior and his early understanding of the rise of social networks. His second book, *Disclosing New Worlds: Entrepreneurship, Democratic Action, and the Cultivation of Solidarity* (MIT Press, 1997), argues that a meaningful life is one of commitment. The major idea in the book is that one's best life is spent "making history," which is defined as pursuing activities that change people's thoughts or behaviors. Key to the potential changes is the opportunity to build trust through meaningful, purposeful, and consistent use of language in all our environments. Firm leaders can add to their positioning strength by taking the time to assess their behaviors and use of language, and then acting to close the gap between what's said and the outcome desired. It can be called "commitment-based management" or "conversations for action," but either way, it's an awareness of the power of what we say, a recognition that most of what we say is a prompt for action. Using language deliberately does come naturally to some people, but for groups in organizations, this task requires more structured guidance, as in the establishment of a set of values.

CASE STUDY: IBM: LESSONS FROM A CORPORATE VALUES JAM

As corporate experiments go, the decision IBM made in 2003 to conduct a 72-hour free-for-all regarding their company's values was a fairly bold risk. IBM had been through some of its toughest times, and was in the middle of a full-scale review of its organization. The Values Jam was intended to engage the entire company in an open debate about the essence of the computer behemoth and what it stood for. Over 10,000 comments were posted on the intranet during that time, most of them not too complimentary. Suggestions to end the experiment were greeted with a stiff refusal from Sam Palmisano, CEO of IBM. He was committed to flushing the system of cynicism and finding answers from his employees that would help return the company to its former glory.

Essentially seeking to find out what was worth preserving and what needed to be changed, executives continued the analysis of the postings and other conversations until they had distilled a strong set of values statements. What resulted wasn't particularly values rocket science, but the credibility factor soared. Executives were asking, and they were listening. According to Palmisano, "We were successful for so long, we could never see another point of view, and when the market shifted, we almost went out of business."

While most firms, large and small, have a difficult time making their values system more than a standard set of feel-good statements, IBM took advantage of a crisis to bring meaning to their effort. After a few drafts were tested and discussed, the new values statements were finalized as follows:

- Dedication to every client's success
- Innovation that matters—for our company and for the world
- Trust and personal responsibility in all relationships

Simple? Yes. Powerful? Absolutely.

Even with a large, far-flung operation like IBM, the values system actually has the power to manage people. When you're in 170 countries and can identify over 100,000 operational "cells," there's no way to control every decision made and action taken. The values system is designed to help keep everyone on the same path, wherever they might be located and whether or not the boss is around. This approach has allowed IBM to begin shifting away from product-driven branding, and begin to make their people the brand. With everyone carrying the same tune in their heads, new strategies can be implemented much more quickly. The employees now realize that *they are* the company, not simply product caretakers.

Facing what many consider a current trend in the design world, IBM also had to address major market and competitive shifts that required it to reintegrate its products and services. During the previous decade or more, the industry had been splintered into hundreds of niche players, each offering its small piece of what the customer wanted. Reintegrating a company as large and complex as IBM required the human underpinning that only a strong set of values could deliver. After the new values statements had been in effect for over a year, here's what Palmisano said about the prognosis:

> We're just starting down the road on what is probably a 10–15 year process. I was back in Asia not long ago, and I did one of those town-hall style meetings with IBM employees and talked about the values. Probably two-thirds of the people clearly knew about them, had read about them. But a third of the people—you could look at their faces and see it—hadn't even heard of the values. Or at least the values hadn't resonated with them yet. So we have work to do. Not just in getting everyone to memorize three pithy statements. We need to do a heck of a lot to close the gaps between our stated values and the reality of IBM today. That's the point of it all. I know that not everyone on my executive team is as enthusiastic about the values initiative as I am—though they'd never admit it! But people on the senior team who lived through IBM's near-death experience will do anything not to go back to that. The blow to everyone's pride when IBM became the laughingstock of the business world was almost too much to bear. I have zero resistance from the senior team on initiatives that can save us from a return to that. And our values work in one of the most important of those initiatives.

The Original Basic Beliefs of IBM:
- Respect for the individual
- The best customer service
- The pursuit of excellence

What began in 1914 when Thomas Watson, Sr., the founder of International Business Machines, dictated the first set of company values, has now come full circle. His three principles, called the Basic Beliefs, could be viewed as perfectly suitable today, even after all these years. But it took a crisis—and the courage to engage the entire staff in an open discussion of who they were as a company—to reestablish a culture held together by a values system that today means something to those who follow it. Sam Palmisano can be proud of his effort, and proud of the fact that IBM can offer its employees something worth believing in and working toward.

From a positioning perspective, values can be considered a "secret sauce" ingredient. It's one thing to have a solid and compelling strategy brought to life through the specifics of how to win the positioning battle. It's another thing to have a firm grasp on the hearts and minds of your staff as you rely on them to execute the plans, across a broad swath of challenges. Time can erode the enthusiasm for a firm's values statements, bringing out the cynical whispers every time someone in a position of leadership makes a misstep. When a firm bands together under a banner of values and makes a strong commitment to live them out, it creates a new sense of mutual responsibility that simply cannot be replaced. Whether the firm is large or small, values can provide a new awareness that brings an extra moment of thought to our decisions and actions. Words count, and all organizations, large and small, have room to discover which words will move the mountains ahead.

MEASURING FOR SUCCESS

The old saw regarding performance measurement states simply, "What gets measured gets done." It's certainly true that all individuals and business entities need multiple forms of feedback to understand where they stand, and more importantly, where they're going.

The accounting and finance universe is filled with a wide variety of terminology and formulas that most firm leaders are familiar with, and many use regularly to assess the status of their business and guide future decisions. These formulas are the ones typical to almost every business, and include items such as the profit and loss (P&L) statement, book value, retained earnings, depreciation, balance sheet, cash flow, and many more. In addition, the design industry has a handful of other measurements that are commonly used to measure performance in a project-oriented environment. These include: net multiplier, overhead rate, utilization rate, net revenue per employee, indirect labor, backlog, and aged accounts receivable, as some of the primary elements. The industry uses other nonfinancial measures with frequency, such as marketing hit rate and staff turnover, plus a few measures that typically relate to budget factors, such as marketing expense and training as a percentage of overall budget. Obviously, there is a wide variance in how these tools are applied, but these are the basics most firms are familiar with.

While most large firms are fully committed to grinding out these rates and formulas on a regular basis, there are still many small and medium-sized firms that take more of a hit-or-miss approach to measuring firm performance. This is a serious mistake when it comes to managing at both the project and firm levels, and continues to severely impact profitability for the firms that don't take this closer look at their operations. When firms step up their commitments to regular performance reporting and analysis, they quite often experience considerable improvements in their overall financial strength. It's basically a Nike thing: "Just do it!®"

Those who have neglected this arena also have an "industry-standard" response as to why they have fallen into that category: "We're too busy." Many times, this response goes along with the sentiment that requiring regular measurement of performance would be considered "too corporate," and might somehow threaten a comfortable culture of what could be called musical chairs of accountability. But since everyone agrees that they'd rather make green than see red when it comes to the bottom line, corporate-style or not, you'll be far ahead if you take the time to track, report, and analyze the important things that the firm is actually doing—and how well they're being done.

A final point in terms of industry standards has to do with benchmarking. The idea behind benchmarking is to use median- and quartile-oriented results compiled from many other firms that are similar to yours in terms of the work you do, your location, your staff size, and so on. Sounds good so far, but this peeking over the neighbor's fence is often encouraged at the front end of a strategic planning process, which should be about your firm's becoming something great, not so much about feeling artificially better or worse because your neighbors make more or less money than you do, or carry more or less debt on their credit cards. It may be more productive to not view benchmarking as a strategic activity. It may be a decent curiosity-driven exercise, but it's much too "averaged out" to be of real use for critical decisions about firm direction and performance. What's more important for a firm is to realize and capture their uniqueness, un-realized ambitions and capabilities, and build a strategy that excites them and carries them along for a good number of years. Once that strategy is developed, they need to measure their own performance, using their previous results or some agreed-on starting point as the real benchmark. This allows them to layer in the realities of their own situation, which may demand high performance in some areas, and allow for less stellar perfor-mance in others, with a clear purpose in mind. This clarity and ownership over the intersection of strategy, performance measurement, and results expectations is the key to taking charge of your future, and a firm can-not afford to be artificially swayed by an aggregation of numbers from many other firms that provide no intelligence about how it was actually created.

New Thinking

Even the latest books about financial management in the design industry spout the same tired stuff; all the old formulas are still there, and there's little or no effort to integrate performance management with strategy and with firm development. This leaves most firms with a small set of worn-out tools and some large gaps and disconnects as they move between their accounting and banking functions and the bigger pictures of strategy, growth, and improved firm performance management.

To further anchor the thinking behind a new approach to measuring for success, baseball offers a great example. The term *sabermetrics* has been in common usage for the past 25 years, and it's a word created from the acronym for the Society of American Baseball Research. Bill James first started publishing his annual baseball abstract in the 1980s, and it soon became the indispensable source of information for professional baseball people as well as fans. With all this data available in one place for the first time, and the advent of cheaper and better computing power, within a number of years a new breed of analyst was devising inventive ways to look at the same old information. Everyone knew about home runs, batting averages, stolen bases, strikeouts, and so on, but who had actually thought about an individual's average performance when it's the eighth inning, two outs, a runner is in scoring position, a lefty is pitching, it's a day game, and it's the batter's birthday? Well, that's essentially what started to happen, and teams like the Oakland Athletics began to develop and use this information to evaluate their players, and assess the worth of other players around the league, for trade and acquisition purposes. (Read *Moneyball* by Michael Lewis for the best in-depth story about this phenomenon.) Interestingly, a new set of information was also being collected, along with new ways of quantifying performance, by looking more closely at some of the intangibles of personality, character, work ethic, and consistency, in order to round out the issues that might arise, beyond the numbers, and have either a positive or negative impact on the team's overall performance. The new measurement game was on. It still is today, and it has turned the art of scouting and statistical analysis into a multidimensional science that is required for every team to remain competitive in their league.

With that model in mind, the design industry has a great opportunity to take a few large evolutionary steps forward in the arena of performance management. Although the historical measures are fine and necessary, they are largely disconnected from strategy, and do not represent the type of integrated information that a twenty-first-century firm needs to manage itself well, keeping ahead of strong competitors. It's time for innovative measurements for design firms, and it's time to bring strategy implementation, systems development, and ongoing operations under the same umbrella, to improve all arenas simultaneously.

Applying the New Thinking

Every firm should build a set of measurements that goes beyond the basics, in order to better understand the complexities and dynamics of their decisions and actions as a team. These measures can typically be organized into four primary categories: marketing, project operations, financial, and administration. Once the firm has chosen and developed its individual measurement focus, these can be blended into a Firm Performance Index that reflects the overall progress of all efforts.

Examples of the types of indices that can be developed, along with some of the possible components, are as follows:

- Revenue Quality Index: Accounts receivable, contract performance, E&O costs, nonbillables, repeat vs. new client revenue, etc.
- Expertise Development Index: Certifications, knowledge management, speaking and writing
- Market Focus Index: Percent of work in chosen markets, by project type
- Product Development Index: Structured services, tools, assessments, handbooks for clients, point-of-entry tools, etc.
- Resources Index: Rate partners by team, rate recruiting performance, rate turnover, expected or not, loss quality rating, key losses reduce rating; resource management ratings—staff allocation, changes, inefficiencies
- Marketing Function Index: Hit rate, lead management, proposal production and quality, placement and support on writing and speaking, PR efforts, direct mail volume, sponsorships, etc.
- Project Management Index: Hours, cost per sheet produced, by project
- Profit Quality Index: Fee leverage, additional scope added, actual to estimate comparisons, etc.
- Design Index: In-house assessment, budget to actual allocation, client assessment, user assessment, etc.
- Growth Index: Geographic reach, revenue and staff growth, etc.

- Client Satisfaction Index: From client surveys, after all medium and large projects with strategic clients
- Culture Index: Staff survey assessment–driven, annual view on issues related to the business, human resources (HR), benefits, office climate, management skills, etc.

These 12 components include hard quantitative, soft quantitative, and a variety of qualitative inputs that should be available within the firm. Key to this measurement system is balance between planning and executing activities, and assessing the quality of the results, both of these planned activities and of the ongoing business of the firm. This is what makes the Firm Performance Index and its components unique and powerful as real tools to track and strengthen your firm's intentions, challenges, and results.

Returning for a moment to the benchmarking idea, the first time a firm begins to use each or any of these indices, that's their benchmark—the point from which they began—and all progress should be measured in relation to that beginning measurement. Of course, as time marches on, the best comparisons will be made year-over-year, quarterly, and monthly.

Looking more closely at the Revenue Quality Index as an example, some of its contributing elements are:

- Contract length, in months
- Projected revenue amount (depending on contract type, use either a fixed or an estimated amount)
- Actual project length
- Accounts receivable performance, in days
- Percent non-billable
- Percent not collectible
- E&O claims paid
- Net project revenue realized
- Risk factor for the project (from an original go/no-go review)

Once the firm has decided on the final mix of elements to make up the index, the next steps are to ensure that consistent sources are available for the necessary data, and then to set up the reporting and analysis frequency that the firm is comfortable with. Keep in mind that there would be weightings applied to each of these elements, depending on what the firm wanted to emphasize. Changes in weightings are a valuable tool to increase focus on particular problem areas as needed.

Expertise Index

Tracking your firm's level of expertise and advancement in relation to key goals and milestones just might represent one of the most important keys to your future. The entire industry talks about knowledge management, market expertise, LEED certification, and the like, but not enough firms turn that casual conversation into a focused program that consolidates the effort into a more powerful achievement. Small and medium-sized firms are especially guilty of leaving things up to the individual staff member, and while that may "feel" right, all too often it doesn't produce the desired results.

The Expertise Index (EI) has a few areas that cross over to the Market Focus Index (MFI), and should be explained. The EI is an overall, firm-wide measurement, and the MFI is measured separately for each strategic market the firm addresses. Non-strategic projects and clients also are tracked within the MFI, but there needs to be a clear separation, as this is critical to overall firm progress as a service provider that is strongly positioned. The EI tracks items such as articles published and speeches given, and it provides credit for these important activities. However, it's not only a matter of getting the speaking or writing accomplished; content value and strength also need to be assessed. This assessment can come from others in the firm, peers, feedback ratings from audience members, and so forth.

Here are examples of the elements that might make up a typical Expertise Index:

- Certifications: Specify type, who, date expected
- Registrations: Specify type, who, date expected
- Articles: By whom, subject, number planned, number actually published, dates, content ratings
- Speeches: By whom, subject, number planned to target markets, actual results; number planned to architect/engineer/contractor (A/E/C) audiences, actual results, including dates, content ratings

For Knowledge Management (KM): Includes seminars attended, in-house KM sessions held, fulfillment of mentoring plans, focused team meetings designed to transfer knowledge and skills, contributions to an in-house newsletter, and the like. This section can be constructed fairly freely within each firm, but the key thing is that specific events be planned, carried out, and recorded in the system in order to receive credit and continue to build a formal record of KM efforts that the firm has taken.

For Proprietary or Customized Research: Includes evidence-based studies, market segment studies, and broad-based client studies related to trends and emerging needs (client feedback on specific projects is captured within the Client Satisfaction Index). Proprietary research involves collecting original findings, analyzing them, and producing a written summary. Customized research involves taking original research from another source, and building on it with your own questions and perspectives, resulting in outcomes you can call your own when speaking to your markets. All research and KM activities are valued according to depth, complexity, and cost, and these elements have appropriately weighted values that affect the final measurements in kind.

While some significant effort can be required to set up a firm-wide measurement system, the payoff can be considerable. Strong measurement systems keep people on their toes, raise the level of communication, and help maintain focus on key strategic and positioning initiatives. Every firm should take a closer look at how they collect and use their performance data, and commit to reaching for new levels of sophistication in this highly creative arena.

CHAPTER 7

ADVANCED RESEARCH AND OPEN INNOVATION

ADVANCED RESEARCH

The term "advanced research" is meant to separate this topic from the basic research that firms engage in when seeking leads or conducting client studies. Conducting advanced research means studying and collecting data in areas that will advance the knowledge and capability of firms and the industry, beyond the immediate goal of procuring the next project. Although the design industry largely relies on outside organizations and associations to provide most of the leadership and muscle for this type of research, the time is arriving when more firms of all sizes, shapes, and budgets will engage in one or more levels of advanced research initiatives. The digital infrastructure, combined with the concept of open innovation, is offering ever greater opportunities to firms that are ready and willing to participate in this process. In addition, increasing competitive pressures will push firms to expand their resumes and networks to include more of this type of experience and engagement.

The essence of advanced research is that it defines the processes that provide new choices, for those in the design industry, and for their clients. As both groups become familiar with the thinking and breakthroughs that lead to new platforms, approaches and applications, the client base will seek out firms that have a history of contributing to and tracking this evolution, whether it's related to energy, sustainable materials, or other areas of development.

Firms wishing to participate in this adventure need to establish some basic principles for their research process. Generically, these principles adhere to a model similar to the following:

- A *commitment* to advanced research that is articulated in the firm's strategy, positioning plan, and values
- A clear *purpose* for this effort, which might be based on societal needs, service to markets, or the betterment of communities
- A willingness to make the *connections* required to join existing circles of activity and influence, or to endeavor to create a new network dedicated to a particular area of study
- A clear intent to *integrate and apply* new processes and approaches as they are discovered or created
- A dedication to client and market *education* regarding the importance of advanced research and the firm's role in creating these contributions

Not all firms will be able to engage in the highest order of research activities, but each firm should consider an effort that stretches their capabilities and resources to the maximum extent available. The following outline illustrates three levels of advanced research activity that firms might seek to achieve.

Level 1: Basic

The firm creates knowledge management circles, rotating various staff through on a periodic basis. Leadership and staff choose topics to focus on, and most of the material is derived from secondary sources collected by the team. Periodic summary reports are generated, along with in-house presentations and seminars. The most salient, well-developed topics are considered for a seminar/presentation to a target client group.

Level 2: Intermediate

The firm develops/recruits thought leaders to deepen the focus on key topics and strategies. Articles, white papers, and presentations are developed to capitalize on the firm's investment, and the firm's positioning story is woven through the research efforts. The firm seeks leadership roles in significant regional, national, and international collaborative research and learning initiatives.

Level 3: Superior

The firm, typically teaming with other providers, conducts original research that contributes to the scientific or analytical advancement of the chosen topic. Research affiliations are formalized with universities, associations, government entities, and the like, with the firm's representatives playing pivotal roles in the group. Grants to further the study of particular topics are applied for.

Although these higher-order efforts may seem lofty, firms will likely find that even a modest amount of exertion in this direction can go a long way. As the Big Shift continues to unfold and expose its opportunities and challenges, the effort devoted to research and innovation in the design industry will expand greatly. New technologies and materials will be developed, requiring integration, and competition will be increasingly driven by specialized firms that know more, and know how to apply their knowledge to maximum benefit. The digital infrastructure is the engine of this new reality, disrupting the status quo with a constant barrage of news, new ideas, and new tools to solve current problems. In the fragmentation of the design world, firms will have to develop the dedication required to keep up with change and innovation, whether by means of their own resources and ingenuity, or through a collaborative arrangement designed to create or gain access to a new competitive advantage. There will be no standing still, no way to rely on outdated information, techniques, or tools and still remain a viable enterprise.

The new face of architecture and engineering will demand that each firm have credible sources of information behind their thinking and design for each and every project. Clients will have the luxury of choosing from a larger number of firms that have invested in research, not only on the topics of sustainability and new materials, but also on trends and developments in the client industry that are reshaping their needs. While some of this research will be available to any firm willing to look for it, more and more firms will be incorporating this intelligence into their own views about its meaning and relevance to clients. For firms that choose not to invest in research, the available sources will be only transactional in nature. Pose a question, seek out a quick answer, choose from a few alternatives, and package it to sell to the client or design into the schematic. This approach, while marginally useful for some issues, won't move the firm's competitive advantage needle very far.

The better model for research and innovation begins with seeking to build long-term, trust-based relationships that feed innovation. Unlike the transactional model, this approach will feed a firm for many years. Consider the open source methodology used by Linux in the corporate world as a good example, and look to engage with other partners and sources in a similar manner.

Research through Dialogue

Gensler is one of the world's foremost expert firms on the workplace, learning environments, and a number of other major markets. They have made it their business to be at the forefront of design and innovation in what otherwise is a very crowded and varied field of focus. Notable in their approach is the stable of platforms and outlets for their perspective and knowledge. Consider their Dialogue product, a compendium of concise insights and opinions that's published in print and online, for free. Key staff members and independent writers from around the world write articles, conduct interviews, and hold round tables with important clients and representatives on that edition's topic. A recent issue focused on "How and Why Universities Grow." An independent writer conducted a round-table discussion with Richard Stanley, senior vice president and university planner at Arizona State University; Nazneen Cooper, assistant dean of physical resources, Faculty of Arts and Sciences at Harvard University; and Dr. Thomas Kail, associate provost and dean of the College of Continuing and Professional Studies at Mercer University. Another example from their collection is an article, also by an independent author, called "Learning Academies," exploring how people learn and covering highlights of topics such as experiential learning, the role of technology, and innovations in schools. You can access over 50 of these articles at gensler.com under the tab Insight, or try dialogue.gensler.com to gain direct access to the Dialogues collection. Through these devices, Gensler is reasserting its leadership role while it attracts new clients and learns from its existing client base. As a basic approach to what could be called "opinion research," it helps provide a platform for thinking about new trends and specific ideas, adding value to conversations both inside and outside the firm. Many firms may not be able to employ independent writers with any frequency, but more firms should be exploring how to put themselves in the center of dialogues that are important to the markets they serve.

End-User Surveys

Another strong device for building a reputation for research-driven thinking is the end-user survey. This may sound similar to conducting a needs assessment related to a new project, but this version is more comprehensive and broader-based. Such a survey can be blended with secondary research from a variety of other sources in the public domain, but more firms should be building a repository of information that their clients are hungry to consume. Consider the survey that WD Partners conducted on millennial dining habits and preferences. The survey was conducted over a six-month period and included over 7,000 respondents aged 18–27. It summarizes both qualitative and quantitative aspects of the research on topics that include socializing, connecting online, establishing a community, frequency of dining, the use of social media, and a range of other important questions. The report also contrasts the millennials with the Baby Boomers, providing an effective way to spot the macro trends from one group to another. As educational and marketing tools, such surveys are powerful, grabbing the attention of clients and allowing for an easy transition to the topics of restaurant design, layout, and overall environment.

Research Collaboration at the University Level

Many universities are looking to forge interdisciplinary partnerships with industry and government. While not every design firm can reach this level of collaboration, there are many more opportunities than there are seekers. Collaboration can start small and exist on an informal basis. Guest lecturing is one method, along with regular attendance at symposia that can generate an informal community of interest among a diverse group of professionals. Moving up the food chain, most larger universities offer programs and guidelines for participation in research projects that are of mutual interest and benefit. As an example, Cornell University publishes guidelines for companies seeking research collaboration. Some of the ways to engage with the university include:

- Sponsor a research project with a particular faculty or group of faculty through the Office of Sponsored Programs.
- Donate funds in the form of a gift for research projects conducted by a particular faculty or within a department, a research center, or laboratory for a specific research project or general area of research.
- Use a research center or laboratory facility on a fee-for-use basis.
- Engage in a comprehensive Strategic Corporate Alliance that involves multiple projects university-wide aligned with strategic business interests.

Each of these options for partnering has different ramifications for a company in terms of the resultant data, any intellectual property, and other results of the project. Certainly, most design firms that would even consider this approach will be starting small. In all likelihood, many firms will be seeking out less formal university connections to develop their network and expand a virtual teaming arrangement. One very effective way to achieve the latter is to hire a university faculty member as a consultant, thereby gaining more direct access to the current level of knowledge and contacts that individual maintains. For many firms, the positioning equation includes increasing credibility on a basis that doesn't necessarily involve specific projects or current clients. University affiliations and activities at almost any level can earn a firm a stronger position as a serious contributor to the profession, and much more should be done to promote and develop this potential.

Another good example is the University of Minnesota College of Design and their Center for Sustainable Building Research. (CSBR) Their mission, as described on their website, www.csbr.umn.edu, is as follows:

> The Center for Sustainable Building Research's mission is to lead and support—through research, outreach, and education—the transformation of the regional built environment to provide for the ecological, economic, and social needs of the present without compromising those of the future.
>
> Conduct and share the research needed to transform the built environment toward sustainability.
>
> Provide assistance and outreach to those working to transform the built environment toward sustainability.
>
> Educate stakeholders in methods for transforming the built environment toward sustainability.
>
> Promote organizational excellence through effective leadership, management, and the establishment of a stable, sustainable base of funding to support our work.

CSBR's list of current and past projects is impressive. Their current project list, as of this writing, consists of the following:

> AIA-CTS: Enhancing Environment and Health in Transportation Project Design
>
> Advanced Energy Efficient Roof System
>
> Awnings in Residential Buildings
>
> Baudette Depot Preservation
>
> Carbon Calculator
>
> City of Saint Paul Green Development Policy
>
> City of Saint Paul Sustainable Building Policy Training Program
>
> Commercial Windows and Glazing
>
> DNR Solar Evaluation Tool

EcoCalculator for Assemblies Tool Development

Hennepin County Energy Recovery Center (HERC) Sustainable Design

Impact of External Shading Devices in Commercial Buildings

Initiative for Renewable Energy in Architecture (reARCH)

Kabetogama Community Center Design Assistance

Midwest Green Building Case Study Project

Minnesota Sustainable Building Guidelines (B3)

Minnesota Sustainable Housing Initiative (MNSHI)

Performance-Based Research on Housing and Infrastructure Development at UMORE Park

Residential Windows and Glazing

Single Family Energy Efficiency Technical Assistance and Verification Program

Solar Daylighting Project

Solar Driven Hydrogen Fuel Cell Demonstration Project

Sustainable Building 2030

Sustainable Housing Research in Korea

Sustainable Post Occupancy Evaluations for Two Washington County Service Centers

Sustainable Shelter—Dwelling Within the Forces of Nature

U of M Solar Decathlon

Viking Terrace Health Outcome Study

CSBR's Archived Project List includes:

DNR Building Evaluation and Design Assistance Project

Duluth Farmers Market Green Design Assistance

Greening CDes

Greening Knowledge Map

HUD COPC: Affordable Housing Initiatives: Case Study Prototypes

Nicollet Meadows Townhomes

Minnesota Green Affordable Housing Guide

Minnesota Sustainable Design Guide (MSDG)

Post Occupancy Evaluations of DNR Area Office Headquarters at Tower & Windom, Minnesota

State Building Database: BRIDGE Project

The Single Family Case Demonstration Project

Sustainable Materials Database

SWMCB Post Occupancy Evaluations

Whether it be in Minnesota or other locales around the country where universities are involved in a similar level of activity that is helping to shape the future, firms need to get closer to the sources that are driving these initiatives. It's time for more firms to discover these resources, devise a strategy to make a connection, learn what's been done, and learn how they can contribute to the next stages of development and accomplishment.

One Firm's Sustainable Lab

A great example of practicing what you preach, LPA Inc.'s Irvine headquarters is located in a building adjacent to the University of California, Irvine (UCI). LPA's commitment in their lease as a tenant in the building was the catalyst for it to be designated as a "Sustainable Design Lab" for UCI's Advanced Power and Energy Program (APEP) on environmental issues. The 28,000-square-foot facility is the first occupied space in California to receive LEED Commercial Interior Certification from the U.S. Green Building Council. The design concentrated on water and energy efficiency, use of recycled materials, disposal of construction waste, and indoor air quality. Many of the green features that were cutting edge in 2003 have become best practices and are good examples of how far and fast sustainability is moving in the design and construction industry.

According to Dan Heinfeld, LPA president, the green workspace was developed as part of a tenant improvement allowance of $30 per square foot in 2003. He adds: "We don't have private offices in the space in order to maximize access to natural daylighting, as well as to promote collaboration." Green housekeeping practices and in-house recycling programs are in place for paper, aluminum, plastics, coffee grounds, and more. There's a highly efficient HVAC, lighting, and electrical system that contributes to an environment that exceeds California's Title 24 energy standards by 22 percent. Recycled materials such as carpet, ceiling tiles, acoustics, fabrics, furniture, and wood were used throughout. The interior materials used consist of 50 percent recycled materials coupled with display signage that highlights recycled materials and products used in the space.

The furniture, designed by LPA, was manufactured within seven miles and blanket-wrapped to reduce carbon emissions and landfill waste. More than 75 percent of all construction waste was recycled and diverted from landfills. Other measures designed to promote a healthy indoor environment include CO_2 monitoring, an indoor air quality (IAQ) plan during construction, and use of low volatile organic compounds (VOC) materials.

Besides the design and construction features, Heinfeld is pleased with the research-related results. In partnership with UCI's Advanced Power and

Energy Program, the National Fuel Cell Research Center, and the South Coast Air Quality Management District, "three 5KW fuel cells have been installed to test the use of smaller cells for onsite generation and heat waste recovery. The natural gas fuel cells produce electricity and the hot water waste used to preheat the space heating requirements for the LPA office."

Heinfeld concludes: "We've also installed a demonstration landscape habitat at the rear of the building using native and drought-tolerant plant materials that eliminate irrigation requirements for this demonstration garden. A bio-swale was also provided in this area so that all stormwater is polished and returned to recharge the groundwater. All in all, having our own sustainability lab environment has allowed the staff to think problems through while working hands-on. It's the kind of space that can really enhance our collaborative efforts, and also provide substantive results that benefit clients and the firm in the long run."

Even if your firm can't develop its own sustainability lab, other sources are plentiful when it comes to advanced research. Membership in the American Solar Energy Society (www.ases.org) should be a must for every firm. The research papers from their conference proceedings can provide the type of in-depth, up-to-date knowledge that your staff needs, and that clients will ultimately pay for in project dollars. The National Renewable Energy Laboratory (nrel.gov) is an outstanding resource that architects and engineers need to utilize and interact with across a broad spectrum of issues. NREL is the only federal laboratory dedicated to the research, development, commercialization, and deployment of renewable energy and energy efficiency technologies.

Back on the private side of the ledger, KieranTimberlake of Philadelphia, Pennsylvania, has recently won the design competition for a solar-powered American embassy in London. They have a long-established research group, and have recognized that research has transformed the firm. Consider the following quote from Steven Kieran as it appeared in ArchDaily in August 2009:

We finally started to realize what was happening to us five years ago in the context of a strategic planning exercise. We really articulated research as the core enterprise that drives the production of the firm. That was an enlightening moment for us. If you ask most firms to diagram what drives them I think you'd find it would be not proactive but rather responsive: what drives them is the work they get. And when we put the research core here—well, part of what we do as researchers is related to questions we need to solve for work that we have to do. It turns the nature of the question around in some ways when you pose it in terms of a research inquiry. It provides a certain amount of rigor to it that is extendable beyond singular circumstance. It's not good enough to put it out there—you have to then monitor what you've done and measure its success and speculate on what you've learned from it.

It cycled for us into a process that also, ironically, became our quality control process. We're ISO (International Organization for Standardization)–certified, one of a relative minority of firms in the U.S. And we didn't think about this at the time, frankly—that the performative requirements of an ISO system exactly parallel research. It's a simple mantra of not just planning and doing things but monitoring and learning from them that is the requirement of our quality control processes. And that's not something we invented. They're used in lots of other industries, and rarely in architecture.

OPEN INNOVATION

The term "open innovation" was coined by Henry Chesbrough, a professor and executive director at the Center for Open Innovation at UC Berkeley, in his book *Open Innovation: The New Imperative for Creating and Profiting from Technology* (Harvard Business School Press, 2003). Open innovation suggests a world where firms use external ideas as well as internal ideas, and seek a variety of pathways to reach their markets. This implies that, as boundaries between a firm and its environment have become more permeable, innovations and the know-how needed to apply them are more readily transferred inward and outward. The primary tenet of open innovation says that companies cannot rely only on their own ideas and research, and should instead trade, buy, or license the ideas of others for their use. Similarly, a company with a valuable idea should be looking for outlets to distribute, license, or otherwise collect value for their effort and discovery. This contrasts with closed innovation, the approach that is now waning, in light of the risks associated with being disconnected from like-minded organizations. Closed innovation can result in a "go it alone" attitude, and quite often, the distance traveled using this approach isn't very far. A firm may hold on to closed innovation out of fear that the competition will find out what they know, or out of simple ignorance about how to go about joining an open innovation cluster. Although keeping sole and secretive control over your ideas may have been a reasonable approach in years past, think about what Procter & Gamble has done. In 1999, they created the position of director of external innovation, mandating that within five years, 50 percent of innovations should come from outside the company. Firms need to discover and contribute to a variety of alliances and networks that will forge long-lasting relationships based on sharing ideas and solutions to today's most pressing problems. With government, universities, industry institutes, and other sources more deeply involved in research and innovation, every firm needs to take advantage of the knowledge and products they are creating. The explosion of technology, combined with the increased pressure of the world's many problems, has created a situation where there is less value in holding on to knowledge. The time has come to join, to contribute, share, and develop knowledge on a more distributed basis for the betterment of every firm, and of society in general. And, as with most important concepts, some principles should be established that begin to organize the thinking around the open innovation concept:

Principles of Open Innovation:

- Mutual interest subject matter
- Multidirectional information flow
- Transparency of purpose and agenda
- Trust
- Commitment to knowledge circulation

The principles in this list can serve as a general guide for firms looking to connect and share what they know, and what they learn. More firms are feeling comfortable with this idea as our industry develops and changes, and this force is only going to grow in size and effect. Think again about a site like http://hoklife.com, discussed in Chapter 5. You'll find any number of examples there and from other firms that are embracing the idea of "giving away" what they know. Ultimately, the purpose of open innovation is to act as an attractor of clients, partners, new staff, and the organizations outside the design world that want to connect with firms that clearly display what they have to offer.

Open innovation can be described as taking advantage of talent that exists beyond the boundary of the firm. As presented by John Hagel III, John Seely Brown, and Lang Davison of The Deloitte Center for The Edge, the relationship model of open innovation is where the real promise lies. Transactional innovation works when explicit knowledge is involved. This requires that problems be precisely framed, and solutions need to be equally precisely stated. However, most of the important problems cannot be framed so precisely. The more challenging problems require accessing the tacit knowledge that resides within a larger group, in order to devise a solution that creates a new level of knowledge. Tacit knowledge is the "know-how" end of the equation that is imprecise, requiring context and situational dimensions in order to become useful. Tacit knowledge also requires working through shared practices, applications on a real project, in order to successfully create solutions that can move beyond surface-level conversations. While many design firms have experience with the virtual teaming demanded by client projects, most do not pursue a model of relationship building that will lead to the accumulation of new levels of knowledge—the levels that lead to true innovation. How many pioneers exist in this arena for design firms to use as a model? If you can name one or two, do you have access to their network and processes? What is the effort that would be required to develop such a process for your firm, and what might the payoff be after five or ten years of experience in open innovation? Answers to these questions at this moment might be thin and uncertain. Yet, the future will be demanding this style of interaction, among firms that thrive in a world of collaborative, creative, and consequential discovery well beyond the standards set by today's institutional gatekeepers. The design industry is fortunate in that there are fewer issues and concerns regarding intellectual property rights and patents than in most industries. We must move beyond the weaker propositions set up by some of the traditional groups whose interests are more aligned with the status quo than with meeting the more volatile dynamics that the Big Shift will continue to deliver. Decide what role your firm should play in the local, regional, or national stage production of open innovation in designing the future.

THE SPARKS FRAMEWORK ASSESSMENT: CHARTING YOUR PREFERENCES

INTRODUCTION TO THE ASSESSMENT

Although some firms find themselves well aligned in terms of strategy, positioning, and practice, many more experience crippling conflicts that sap the energy of the organization. They fall victim to the prevailing one-size-fits-all advice, such as "grow or die," "diversify to hedge your bets," "be 'problem solvers' who chase anything," "get cheaper," "be more flexible," and "go global," among many of the popular solutions one might name.

The SPARKS Framework Assessment, developed and originally published by Ellen Flynn-Heapes, is a succinct decision-making tool for helping firm leaders craft a clear, integrated business model that generates value and builds high client esteem. The assessment tool is the product of over 15 years of research into the most successful firms in the industry. The framework is organized into six cultural archetypes, loosely based on the six heroic archetypes of Swiss psychologist Carl Jung, as discussed in *Creating Wealth: Principles and Practices for Design Firms*, also by Ellen Flynn-Heapes. Each archetype is defined by distinctive best practices in 20 specific categories.

The assessment helps leaders understand past choices and thoughtfully consider options for the future, using the master archetypes as a baseline of comparison. Not only does the assessment help highlight inconsistencies within a firm's current model, but it also paints a vivid picture of the gaps between current practice and the future vision. The assessment, when used by all members of the leadership team, becomes the ideal staging ground for truly excellent strategic planning and positioning work.

With an eye toward making your firm more distinctive in the marketplace, you must first design your practice around your strengths, and then purposefully and confidently act in concert with your design. This is the fundamental lesson of leadership, and the basic principle of creating wealth.

WHO SHOULD PARTICIPATE IN THE ASSESSMENT?

Firms use the assessment to gain wide input from principals, managers, key staff, and sometimes even favorite clients, to prepare for company strategy retreats. This participative effort pays off in better information, enhanced consensus building, and ultimately, implementation.

Firms also use this tool to test the waters for a cultural and strategic match prior to mergers and acquisitions, strategic alliance partnerships, and the lateral hiring of senior personnel.

INSTRUCTIONS

The survey should take about 20–30 minutes to complete. It requires you to choose the single most fitting of six current and six future scenarios for your firm, in 20 key areas of operation. Fill out the survey according to your personal views about your firm. For each question, indicate your view of current practice, using *only one check in the Current column*, and indicate any changes for the future, using *only one check in the Future column*.

These scenarios often overlap in everyday practice. However, in most cases one choice will ring more true for your firm than the others. Responses to these 20 questions, when correlated, will chart both alignment and areas of conflict in your business design. When the picture becomes clear, the course of action becomes clear. And remember, there are no incorrect answers, only inconsistencies.

Teams wishing to fully utilize the assessment tool will need to purchase copies of the booklet for individual worksheets and the scoring of results. Please visit www.forsparks.com for ordering information.

Sample:

A.	In the marketplace, our firm is known for (select one current and one future answer):	Current	Future
1.	Developing new, cutting edge ideas that are not necessarily specific to any one project type.		
2.	Mastery of our niche within a broader industry. We have specialized expertise in a project or service type.		✓
3.	Our experience within a broader industry or client type. We sometimes call in niche experts for specific project requirements.	✓	
4.	Our contribution and relationships within our community or geographic locale.		
5.	Our project management and organizational skills on complex and/or multiple projects, emphasizing control and speed.		
6.	Our expertise at saving our clients money through our outstanding production processes.		

THE SPARKS FRAMEWORK ASSESSMENT: TWENTY CRITICAL CHOICES FOR FIRM LEADERS

A.	Our image and reputation in the marketplace are best described as (select one current and one future answer):	Current	Future
1.	A firm that creates cutting-edge ideas and new theories. May be R&D leaders in engineering, or avant-garde leaders in architecture.		
2.	A firm with deep expertise in a singular project-type or service-type niche within a specific industry.		
3.	A firm with broad experience in one or a few targeted industries or markets. Sometimes brings in niche experts for technical or specialty needs.		
4.	A firm that contributes to the local community and has strong relationships with others in the public and private sectors who also contribute.		
5.	A firm with great project management and organizational skills that it brings to complex projects.		
6.	A firm that can really save its clients money.		

B.	We are hired especially because of our ability to (select one current and one future answer):	Current	Future
1.	Catapult our clients to the cutting edge. By improving their prestige and image as leaders, we help them attract *their* target audiences, who tend to be looking for something special.		
2.	Bring the deepest, most current knowledge and experience to bear on specific aspects of highly visible, complex, risky private-sector and public-sector projects.		
3.	Be fully a part of the client's team, as if we were integrated into their organization. Since we're a major player in their industry, they're confident that we know their needs. We offer the range of services under our roof, being prepared for virtually any kind of project work within their area of interest.		
4.	Facilitate the project through local gatekeepers. Our "insider" presence in the social and political environment greases the wheels for acceptance of our client's projects.		
5.	Manage large, highly complex, logistically challenging projects or programs, including design/build work.		
6.	Deliver the product, optimizing the budget. Our work is consistent and high quality, often including prototype/site-adapt projects at lower costs than our competitors.		

C.	Our favorite projects are (select one current and one future answer):	Current	Future
1.	Those where we can be a little radical in our expression of what can be done to meet the client's needs. Sometimes what comes out is a surprise to everyone.		
2.	Those where we've applied the latest innovations in our area of focus to both stimulate and meet the client's needs. We've advanced everyone's thinking and we've delivered a better end product.		
3.	The next project for our favorite clients with whom we have a long-term relationship. Certainly we take pride in our work, but we feel satisfied when our client sees us as a trusted, integral part of their team.		
4.	The most important, most visible jobs in our community. Although we tend to team with out-of-towners for the specialty stuff, we're seen locally as the firm in charge of the team.		
5.	The complex projects with lots of puzzle pieces and loose ends to be tied up neatly. Our clients rely on us to manage the mess.		
6.	Those where we've saved the client lots of time and money. They view us as real contributors to their bottom line, which is of utmost importance.		

D.	Our sales activities are led by (select one current and one future answer):	Current	Future
1.	Creative, thought-provoking guru(s), who inspire and stretch their clients intellectually with their bold ideas.		
2.	Niche experts with deep expertise in a specialized area who live and breathe their specific project- or service-type knowledge.		
3.	Principals with broad knowledge and involvement in our chosen client type or sector, a few of whom have had earlier careers on the client side.		
4.	Principals and/or office managers who are well known locally and committed to the protection and prosperity of the community.		
5.	Senior project managers, often VPs, who are well compensated for revenue generation and project profitability.		
6.	A professional sales manager or marketing director with a cadre of sharp sales reps.		

E.	Our promotional efforts emphasize (select one current and one future answer):	Current	Future
1.	Teaching, awards, and visibility in professional publications recognizing our ideas.		
2.	Seminars at client conferences and articles in the client press displaying advances in our niche expertise.		
3.	Networking and market-specific brochures and newsletters targeted within our client type or industry.		
4.	Participation in local community groups, coverage in local newspapers, radio talk shows, social and political sponsorship of community events.		
5.	Press coverage in the general business press; professional "annual report" illustrating the scope and complexity of our projects.		
6.	High-quality direct-mail and advertising programs; well-designed exhibit booths at client trade shows.		

F.	Our project teams are led by (select one current and one future answer):	Current	Future
1.	Pioneers and creative idea innovators, with support from design teams to make concepts "real."		
2.	Niche-dedicated leaders, applying ideas pragmatically through a team, some of whom may be from outside the firm in alliances.		
3.	Seasoned principals with a broad knowledge of how their sector operates; supported by similarly dedicated PMs and teams.		
4.	Local principals or office managers. Support from other discipline leads, whether local or drawn from other offices, if multi-office.		
5.	Senior PMs with support from assistant PMs to help manage project logistics.		
6.	PMs who supervise production teams, with support from senior technicians and production staff.		

G.	Our project management process is best characterized by (select one current and one future answer):	Current	Future
1.	Patient, flexible individuals who adapt to the leader's individual interests and approach.		
2.	Dedicated niche experts who can also handle the realities of the management process. Although we focus on pushing the envelope in our specialty, we are clever about using new technologies to save us time.		
3.	Individuals who are most experienced in our chosen market(s). Project management is a challenging role in the firm, with pretty good procedures in place. We sometimes send people to seminars for training.		
4.	The locally connected principal who sold the job as chief PM (and possibly even designer, depending on project size). Production by staff members; may include multiple disciplines.		
5.	Very strong project managers, as well as innovative company-wide PM systems and procedures applied to varying large-scale project types.		
6.	Clearly accountable (and incentivized) PMs, with emphasis on the rigorous use and updating of systems, procedures, and details.		

H.	Our most valued use of computer technology is (select one current and one future answer):	Current	Future
1.	Enhancing visualization and supporting constructibility. If science-based, helping us experiment with new technological processes, models, etc.		
2.	Supporting development and visualization of next-generation improvements. Also having a base from which to make changes more easily.		
3.	Producing good, accurate documents that do the job, protect us from future liability problems, and provide a base for follow-on work with the client.		
4.	Client database "dossiers" that let us keep track of local people, politics, and projects.		
5.	Project planning, scheduling, and managing the logistics of our complex projects.		
6.	Production-oriented, streamlining our systems, and fine-tuning our tools and details so we can break the cost barrier.		

I.	Our favorite discussions tend to emphasize (select one current and one future answer):	Current	Future
1.	Original approaches, brainstorming, and creative ideas.		
2.	Next-generation evolution; how to apply newly minted ideas to our niche.		
3.	Latest developments, news, trends, players, projects, competitors, regulations, etc. within our clients' environment.		
4.	Local news of clients, competitors, and newsworthy events affecting our community. Some complaints about how much the principals are absent—too much emphasis on their extracurricular activities on local boards, etc.		
5.	Project management trends and techniques affecting coordination, speed, and performance.		
6.	Techniques re: productivity, production tools, technologies, and TQM.		

J.	Our leading employees tend to come from (select one current and one future answer):	Current	Future
1.	Academia, often prestigious design institutions.		
2.	Strong universities, other same-niche-focused competitors, and selected generalist firms whose staff members want to specialize.		
3.	Mainstream universities, similarly client- or industry-focused design firms, and sometimes directly from clients.		
4.	Local and state universities and colleges, other local firms, and local government client agencies.		
5.	Business schools, often after a design degree.		
6.	Local colleges and technical schools.		

K.	Our staff mix consists of (select one current and one future answer):	Current	Future
1.	A few original thinkers at the top and mid-levels, including PhDs, with selected bright recruits eager to "continue their education" and have us on their resume.		
2.	Specialists at top project levels, along with dedicated young professionals who aspire to gain niche knowledge.		
3.	Industry-focused career professionals at the top, some from our client industry, balanced with mid-career and younger professionals.		
4.	Well-connected community players, balanced with mid-career and younger professionals. Mid-career professionals often head various in-house disciplines.		
5.	A cadre of senior project managers and a larger staff of strong technical professionals with specific project team responsibilities.		
6.	A few senior project team leaders, leveraged by a substantial staff of junior professionals and technicians.		

L.	Our staff's career growth is spurred by (select one current and one future answer):	Current	Future
1.	Challenging the guru to think even more creatively, and contributing significant energy and enthusiasm to the cause. Learning often occurs informally with the guru after hours.		
2.	Acquiring niche expertise quickly, working long hours, and actively seeking a mentoring relationship.		
3.	Learning the issues and operations of our target client group, attending market-specific seminars, and taking advantage of informal mentoring by senior staff.		
4.	Attending local seminars, networking at Chamber of Commerce events and professional association meetings, and being active in the community.		
5.	Bringing in profitable results. Also capitalizing on the firm's "university" training curriculum and outside MBA programs.		
6.	Efficiency, high productivity, and seniority. Learning improves with formal training programs and classes.		

M.	Our approach to compensation is to (select one current and one future answer):	Current	Future
1.	Share profits and bonuses as they become available, mostly to gurus and enabling management. Junior staff are rewarded through learning and the prestige.		
2.	Provide above-average salaries across the board to mostly high-level personnel. Bonuses are distributed on a subjective basis to those with high dedication and special expertise.		
3.	Provide average salaries at all levels. Bonus pool is distributed according to position and performance within industry-practice groups.		
4.	Set salaries of principals modestly, and—depending on strength of local economy and effectiveness of strategies—give commensurate bonuses. If multi-office, bonus pool depends on branch-office performance.		
5.	Give high salaries at the top. Well-articulated performance-oriented compensation systems for PMs.		
6.	Give high salaries and bonuses at the top for client managers and supervisors. Wage rates are "by the book" with incentive programs for productivity.		

N.	Beyond the fundamental "golden rule" personal values and the basic business values of marketing and profitability, the most important value that drives our firm is (select one current and one future answer):	Current	Future
1.	Innovation, creativity, and originality of ideas.		
2.	"Product" leadership; advancing the state-of-the-art in our specialty.		
3.	Client intimacy; partnership; long-term relationships with key clients.		
4.	Involvement, contribution, and deep connections in our community.		
5.	Project management excellence; the challenge of the project chess game.		
6.	Elegant efficiency; stamping out waste; saving our clients money.		

O.	Our pricing is based on (select one current and one future answer):	Current	Future
1.	Perceived value and prestige that our design reputation brings to the project.		
2.	Confidence value of our niche expertise and documented results from previous projects.		
3.	Cost of the work and market rates; our profit improves when the firm works with higher-end repeat clients and industry referrals.		
4.	Cost of the work and market rates; our profit improves with networked relationships and lower marketing overhead. If multi-office, may capitalize on headquarters/branch price differentials.		
5.	Negotiated fees; our profit improves with well-managed incentive fees, e.g. early delivery.		
6.	Unit pricing; our profit improves with increased productivity and efficiency relative to the bid/proposal.		

P.	Beyond the financial reporting basics, our management information system is focused on tracking (select one current and one future answer):	Current	Future
1.	Nothing else.		
2.	Benefit statistics of our niche-type design effectiveness.		
3.	Revenue and profitability by industry-based business units and segments within units. Also revenue from repeat clients.		
4.	Revenue and profitability by geographic office.		
5.	Project profitability, labor scheduling, and reporting.		
6.	Production unit costs and production group profitability.		

Q.	When it comes to growth, we invest our financial resources in developing (select one current and one future answer):	Current	Future
1.	Fresh ideas and experiments, as well as adding to our cadre of the best minds available in order to stimulate development of new ideas.		
2.	New opportunities for applying and advancing our expertise. Also, growth of our network of partners for complementary full services and cross-selling.		
3.	Bench depth in target industry experience, including strategic hires from client organizations. Also acquisition of other same-market practices.		
4.	Public relations to maintain visibility as the top firm in our locale. Also creating a network of national experts to bring in for more complex projects. If multi-office, acquisition of new well-connected local players. We sometimes invest in local real estate ventures.		
5.	An elite corps of well-trained project managers and management systems, as well as a network of local alliances for representation at local sites.		
6.	Increased production capacity, improved equipment, and partnerships with clients and design firms for their volume-oriented work.		

R.	Our firm is owned by (select one current and one future answer):	Current	Future
1.	One or a few design- and/or research-oriented principals.		
2.	A small group of distinguished product- or service-type niche experts.		
3.	Well-known industry design leaders and a very select group of proven technical experts.		
4.	A broad group of office, discipline, and corporate leaders. May be an ESOP.		
5.	An infrastructure of key leaders at the top, most often current or former senior PMs; has a "corporate" feel.		
6.	One or a few entrepreneurs; can be corporate or family-owned.		

S.	Our internal organizational structure is organized around (select one current and one future answer):	Current	Future
1.	Highly creative individuals with special interests. Loosely structured to optimize new ideas.		
2.	Niche-specific experts to optimize advancement in the niche.		
3.	One or a few industry-type "practice groups" to optimize market expertise. In some cases, practice groups may incorporate related niche experts.		
4.	Local leaders/personalities who optimize connectivity, and discipline leaders to optimize production capabilities.		
5.	Project managers and their large projects to optimize PM systems and technologies.		
6.	Project departments or dedicated production teams to optimize productivity and efficiency.		

T.	Our best physical configuration is (select one current and one future answer):	Current	Future
1.	Single office for critical mass of idea generation. May sometimes deploy special research/or design teams to their own separate space for focused project development.		
2.	One primary office base for enhancing new applications of ideas. Our "out-of-town experts" travel. We enjoy a true "distribution" network of alliances and partnerships.		
3.	A select few "equal" offices to strategically serve our client industry's needs regionally or nationally.		
4.	One or more full-service offices designed to be physically near our clients, often in smaller municipalities. Central administrative office and/or regional clustering.		
5.	Corporate headquarters and offices in larger municipalities. PMs travel and may relocate temporarily to key project locations.		
6.	One primary production and administrative center, with marketing and field support offices as necessary to penetrate markets.		

AFTERWORD

THE FUTURE OF THE DESIGN PROFESSION

Anyone who sees things primarily in terms of systems has experienced a flood of thoughts and reactions, during the past few years, as the economic health of the entire world has approached the limits of its capabilities. Times like these are sobering and frightening, but also full of possibilities.

Certain categories of engineering have suffered greatly, but it's the architectural profession that has really taken it on the chin. According to the Bureau of Labor Statistics (BLS), the peak of architectural employment was reached in July 2009 at 224,500. By November of 2009, it had dropped by 40,000, and it continues to shrink, without quick recovery in sight. For the full year, employment among architects declined by 17.8 percent, with construction spending for 2010 predicted to fall another 13.4 percent, according to the AIA's Consensus Construction Forecast, released in early 2010. In the BLS Occupational Outlook Handbook, 2010–2011 edition, which includes a look at the architectural industry, the following predictions were made:

> TRENDS FOR THE FUTURE: The bureau projects that employment is likely to grow faster than the average for all occupations. This means growth can be expected, particularly at more prestigious firms.
>
> EMPLOYMENT CHANGE: The bureau projects employment of architects to increase 16 percent by 2018.
>
> OUTSOURCING: Some firms have outsourced the drafting of construction documents and basic design for large-scale commercial and residential projects overseas, the bureau notes. It expects this to continue, which could have a negative impact on growth for lower-level architects and interns who gain experience by doing this work.
>
> JOB PROSPECTS: Competition is expected to remain, as a growing number of graduates enter the work force. Entry-level jobs are likely to have the most competition.
>
> GREEN DESIGN: The bureau touts green design as an increasingly important tool, noting that there "should be demand" for architects with such knowledge.

One might suspect that the rosier predictions for employment growth through 2018 are based on older models that aren't equipped to deal with the severe financial changes many countries will have to make to stay solvent over that period. However, one of the most intriguing parts of the report has to do with the idea that "growth can be expected, particularly at more prestigious firms." While the definition of "prestigious" is debatable, the idea seems correct. Larger firms that have substantial capabilities, deep market penetration, and the ability to weather economic cycles will take a larger share of the market as the decades wear on. Without the free-and-easy flow of funds that was available in recent decades, clients will demand higher levels of predictable performance that only the larger firms can consistently deliver. Small and medium-sized firms, without clear specialization to strengthen their value, will be relegated to run-of-the-mill projects where making significant profits will be difficult.

Words like "survival" and "recovery" tend to become the hooks we hang onto during periods of uncertainty such as these, and while that's a normal human response, it isn't likely to get the job done this time around. This time, a more holistic shift is necessary, to redefine our purpose and redesign a number of industries, including architecture. Over the last 30 years, our country, along with most of the developed world, has been balancing on a false-bottomed creation of credit, debt, and other tools of financial risk—and the bottom has now fallen out. This financial shortfall is likely to remain in effect for generations to come, but it is not the only crisis produced by our social, corporate, and individual decisions; at the same time, we have become aware that our planet needs some serious help. Yet most leaders of industry, the professions, and government are limiting their view of what needs changing and how to go about it. This continued use of conventional thinking within outmoded systems is not only ineffective, it's a direct threat to the historical greatness of America and much of the developed world.

Now that we've reached this nadir, can we afford to believe that everything will turn out fine, as long as the rest of the world follows in our footsteps? Democracy itself aside, what have we learned about free markets and consumerism? How can those lessons guide our design of an economic system that won't carry us to the edge of disaster? In a country built upon the ideal of endless possibility, will we be able to maintain our essential political fabric if these limitless horizons begin to shrink? These issues are obviously too serious for the typical hopes for survival and recovery that saw the economy through previous slowdowns. It was relatively painless to work around those misalignments of supply and demand/inventory, and then we were off to the races again. Not this time.

The larger questions at stake include the direction of society itself, and architects certainly need to think deeply about their role within the new context that has emerged. The dangers to this process are ego, self-preservation tactics, and the simple inability to conceive of new uses for professional training. For those caught in that web, the next decades will be very unsatisfying. For those able to free themselves of the constraints that require a return to the way things were, the possibilities are real and quite exciting.

Six Rules

Here are six new rules for designers to consider when it comes to shaping their future role in the world:

- *It's time to go broader (services) and deeper (markets).* Architects need to overcome the limitation of thinking that they only design buildings. That skill will represent one service among many in the future design firm. More serious attention needs to be paid to societal design, environmental design, and the creation of multidisciplinary solutions of which architecture is only one piece. Logically, design firms should consist of many disciplines under one roof. These may include all the traditional services offered by a typical A/E firm, plus: financial planning, organizational design and development, technology consulting, market research, strategic planning, product design, process development, and an entire array of other services to choose from. However, as the list of services gets broader, the market focus needs to become sharper, deeper. More large professional services firms will emerge with a powerful set of tools for a specific industry. It's not that stand-alone design firms won't have any facility-design work coming their way—it's more that the criteria for obtaining this work will demand a different version of design firm—one that has developed a longer-term, multifaceted relationship with the owner.
- *Consider either moving away from production or embracing it as your primary purpose.* No one service firm can perform all functions equally well. The varying orientation of the leaders and the resulting compromise of purpose dilute the entire process, and the world urgently needs higher performance across the spectrum. Think of this forced choice as a means to achieve professional satisfaction and success, using the following three elements:
  - Client/market knowledge and depth of expertise
  - Problem solving and design application
  - Design production

  The first element represents the new world of integrated, holistic thinking that all clients will be seeking to access as a new array of systems begins to take shape. A firm that performs this function well won't be focused on managing the day-to-day aspects of producing final drawings. The problem-solving and design application role is the hinge, and a firm can see it in one of two ways: It's the front end of the design production service, or it's the back end of the interdisciplinary market expertise. If you choose the knowledge expert approach, you'll need to be satisfied without producing a physical facility. Satisfaction will come from having the best information and approach to ROI analysis, life-cycle planning, and operational performance.

- *Change the measurement of growth.* For years, architects have measured growth primarily in terms of staff size and total revenues. For future production-driven firms, success will be measured in efficiency, accuracy, quality, and timeliness. Expert knowledge firms will need to measure the growth in their knowledge base, solution frameworks, and client satisfaction. The ultimate scenario will contain fewer but larger production firms, and potentially more but smaller knowledge firms.

- *Future design will be driven primarily by essential functions plus harmony with nature.* The epoch of purely ego-driven design-by-imagination is largely over for the foreseeable future. Future design will be more grounded in aesthetics, and more directly connected to purpose and function. Its beauty will be in the way it acknowledges and celebrates nature and humankind as one, instead of indulging in a more haphazard use of space, materials, or human potential. Design elements will need to be more well-integrated into the building's orientation and systems than in the past.

- *Restorative planning will drive communities.* Recycling will take on larger proportions and a greater purpose. Instead of abandoning older, worn-out parts of our towns and cities, we will be forced to reuse them until we discover how beautiful the results are, and how well this allows our new societal system to function. Developers will no longer rule the skyline, the politics, and the flow of money that has often resulted in the destruction of important places and the creation of places without a soul.

- *BIM and other integrative tools will become the only acceptable way to execute projects.* Holistic tools that engage the entire team, ensure efficiency, centralize responsibility, and reduce waste and errors will arrive as the norm very soon. As the industry struggles to redefine its purpose and role, clients will push to reduce the costs of design, along with the inefficiencies of teams that only pretend to be on the same page.

The era of waste, indulgence, and isolation within the entire process of design and construction is over. Firms of the future are taking shape now, writing the new rules for how the industry will function and behave. The new beliefs and approaches will result in a fairly drastic rearrangement of the industry, followed by a resurgence of the profession to prominence. Yet, there are a number of "ifs" attached to that possibility: *If* design professionals of all types learn how to build value in different ways, they will succeed. *If* they apply a better set of tools to their problems and challenges, they will prevail. And *if* they learn the meaning of collaboration at a more essential level, they will thrive.

Individual firms will need to become more integrated, capable of offering a bona fide full-service approach to clients. Teams that come together for a project will need to already share common platforms for technology, change management, value engineering, and commissioning. The future is bright, but it looks quite different from the past. With a sharper focus, more attention paid to efficiency, and some fastening of seat belts, it can and will be a great ride.

INDEX